ARTHRITIS

THE ENCYCLOPEDIA OF
HEALTH

MEDICAL DISORDERS AND THEIR TREATMENT

Dale C. Garell, M.D. · General Editor

ARTHRITIS

Mary C. Powers

Introduction by C. Everett Koop, M.D., Sc.D.
former Surgeon General, U. S. Public Health Service

CHELSEA HOUSE PUBLISHERS

New York · Philadelphia

The goal of the ENCYCLOPEDIA OF HEALTH *is to provide general information in the ever-changing areas of physiology, psychology, and related medical issues. The titles in this series are not intended to take the place of the professional advice of a physician or other health care professional.*

CHELSEA HOUSE PUBLISHERS
EDITOR-IN-CHIEF   Remmel Nunn
MANAGING EDITOR   Karyn Gullen Browne
COPY CHIEF   Mark Rifkin
PICTURE EDITOR   Adrian G. Allen
ART DIRECTOR   Maria Epes
ASSISTANT ART DIRECTOR   Howard Brotman
MANUFACTURING DIRECTOR   Gerald Levine
SYSTEMS MANAGER   Lindsey Ottman
PRODUCTION MANAGER   Joseph Romano
PRODUCTION COORDINATOR   Marie Claire Cebrián

The Encyclopedia of Health
SENIOR EDITOR   Brian Feinberg

Staff for ARTHRITIS
ASSOCIATE EDITOR   LaVonne Carlson-Finnerty
COPY EDITOR   Ian Wilker
EDITORIAL ASSISTANT   Tamar Levovitz
PICTURE RESEARCHER   Toby Greenberg
DESIGNER   Robert Yaffe

First Printing
1   3   5   7   9   8   6   4   2

Library of Congress Cataloging-in-Publication Data

Powers, Mary C.
   Arthritis/by Mary C. Powers; introduction by C. Everett Koop.
      p. cm.—(The Encyclopedia of health. Medical disorders and their treatment)
   Includes bibliographical references and index.
   Summary: An examination of the many types of arthritis and the methods used to releive this painful, often crippling disease.
   ISBN 0-7910-0057-5
         0-7910-0484-8 (pbk.)
   1. Arthritis—Juvenile literature. [1. Arthritis.] I. Title. II. Series.   91-34165
RC933.P63 1992   CIP
616.7'22—dc20   AC

CONTENTS

THE HEALTHY BODY

THE LIFE CYCLE

MEDICAL ISSUES

PSYCHOLOGICAL DISORDERS AND THEIR TREATMENT

MEDICAL DISORDERS AND THEIR TREATMENT

PREVENTION AND EDUCATION: THE KEYS TO GOOD HEALTH

C. Everett Koop, M.D., Sc.D.
former Surgeon General,
U.S. Public Health Service

The issue of health education has received particular attention in recent years because of the presence of AIDS in the news. But our response to this particular tragedy points up a number of broader issues that doctors, public health officials, educators, and the public face. In particular, it points up the necessity for sound health education for citizens of all ages.

Over the past 25 years this country has been able to bring about dramatic declines in the death rates for heart disease, stroke, accidents, and for people under the age of 45, cancer. Today, Americans generally eat better and take better care of themselves than ever before. Thus, with the help of modern science and technology, they have a better chance of surviving serious—even catastrophic—illnesses. That's the good news.

But, like every phonograph record, there's a flip side, and one with special significance for young adults. According to a report issued in 1979 by Dr. Julius Richmond, my predecessor as Surgeon General, Americans aged 15 to 24 had a higher death rate in 1979 than they did 20 years earlier. The causes: violent death and injury, alcohol and drug abuse, unwanted pregnancies, and sexually transmitted diseases. Adolescents are particularly vulnerable because they are beginning to explore their own sexuality and perhaps to experiment with drugs. The need for educating young people is critical, and the price of neglect is high.

Yet even for the population as a whole, our health is still far from what it could be. Why? A 1974 Canadian government report attributed all death and disease to four broad elements: inadequacies in the health care system, behavioral factors or unhealthy life-styles, environmental hazards, and human biological factors.

To be sure, there are diseases that are still beyond the control of even our advanced medical knowledge and techniques. And despite yearnings that are as old as the human race itself, there is no "fountain of youth" to ward off aging and death. Still, there is a solution to many of the problems that undermine sound health. In a word, that solution is prevention. Prevention, which includes health promotion and education, saves lives, improves the quality of life, and in the long run, saves money.

In the United States, organized public health activities and preventive medicine have a long history. Important milestones in this country or foreign breakthroughs adopted in the United States include the improvement of sanitary procedures and the development of pasteurized milk in the late 19th century and the introduction in the mid-20th century of effective vaccines against polio, measles, German measles, mumps, and other once-rampant diseases. Internationally, organized public health efforts began on a wide-scale basis with the International Sanitary Conference of 1851, to which 12 nations sent representatives. The World Health Organization, founded in 1948, continues these efforts under the aegis of the United Nations, with particular emphasis on combating communicable diseases and the training of health care workers.

Despite these accomplishments, much remains to be done in the field of prevention. For too long, we have had a medical care system that is science- and technology-based, focused, essentially, on illness and mortality. It is now patently obvious that both the social and the economic costs of such a system are becoming insupportable.

Implementing prevention—and its corollaries, health education and promotion—is the job of several groups of people.

First, the medical and scientific professions need to continue basic scientific research, and here we are making considerable progress. But increased concern with prevention will also have a decided impact on how primary care doctors practice medicine. With a shift to health-based rather than morbidity-based medicine, the role of the "new physician" will include a healthy dose of patient education.

Second, practitioners of the social and behavioral sciences— psychologists, economists, city planners—along with lawyers, business leaders, and government officials—must solve the practical and ethical dilemmas confronting us: poverty, crime, civil rights, literacy, education, employment, housing, sanitation, environmental protection, health care delivery systems, and so forth. All of these issues affect public health.

Third is the public at large. We'll consider that very important group in a moment.

Fourth, and the linchpin in this effort, is the public health profession—doctors, epidemiologists, teachers—who must harness the professional expertise of the first two groups and the common sense and cooperation of the third, the public. They must define the problems statistically and qualitatively and then help us set priorities for finding the solutions.

To a very large extent, improving those statistics is the responsibility of every individual. So let's consider more specifically what the role of the individual should be and why health education is so important to that role. First, and most obvious, individuals can protect themselves from illness and injury and thus minimize their need for professional medical care. They can eat nutritious food; get adequate exercise; avoid tobacco, alcohol, and drugs; and take prudent steps to avoid accidents. The proverbial "apple a day keeps the doctor away" is not so far from the truth, after all.

Second, individuals should actively participate in their own medical care. They should schedule regular medical and dental checkups. Should they develop an illness or injury, they should know when to treat themselves and when to seek professional help. To gain the maximum benefit from any medical treatment that they do require, individuals must become partners in that treatment. For instance, they should understand the effects and side effects of medications. I counsel young physicians that there is no such thing as too much information when talking with patients. But the corollary is the patient must know enough about the nuts and bolts of the healing process to understand what the doctor is telling him or her. That is at least partially the patient's responsibility.

Education is equally necessary for us to understand the ethical and public policy issues in health care today. Sometimes individuals will encounter these issues in making decisions about their own treatment or that of family members. Other citizens may encounter them as jurors in medical malpractice cases. But we all become involved, indirectly, when we elect our public officials, from school board members to the president. Should surrogate parenting be legal? To what extent is drug testing desirable, legal, or necessary? Should there be public funding for family planning, hospitals, various types of medical research, and other medical care for the indigent? How should we allocate scant technological resources, such as kidney dialysis and organ transplants? What is the proper role of government in protecting the rights of patients?

What are the broad goals of public health in the United States today? In 1980, the Public Health Service issued a report aptly entitled *Promoting Health—Preventing Disease: Objectives for the Nation*. This report expressed its goals in terms of mortality and in terms of intermediate goals in education and health improvement. It identified 15 major concerns: controlling high blood pressure; improving family planning; improving pregnancy care and infant health; increasing the rate of immunization; controlling sexually transmitted diseases; controlling the presence of toxic agents and radiation in the environment; improving occupational safety and health; preventing accidents; promoting water fluoridation and dental health; controlling infectious diseases; decreasing smoking; decreasing alcohol and drug abuse; improving nutrition; promoting physical fitness and exercise; and controlling stress and violent behavior.

For healthy adolescents and young adults (ages 15 to 24), the specific goal was a 20% reduction in deaths, with a special focus on motor vehicle injuries and alcohol and drug abuse. For adults (ages 25 to 64), the aim was 25% fewer deaths, with a concentration on heart attacks, strokes, and cancers.

Smoking is perhaps the best example of how individual behavior can have a direct impact on health. Today, cigarette smoking is recognized as the single most important preventable cause of death in our society. It is responsible for more cancers and more cancer deaths than any other known agent; is a prime risk factor for heart and blood vessel disease, chronic bronchitis, and emphysema; and is a frequent cause of complications in pregnancies and of babies born prematurely, underweight, or with potentially fatal respiratory and cardiovascular problems.

Since the release of the Surgeon General's first report on smoking in 1964, the proportion of adult smokers has declined substantially, from 43% in 1965 to 30.5% in 1985. Since 1965, 37 million people have quit smoking. Although there is still much work to be done if we are to become a "smoke-free society," it is heartening to note that public health and public education efforts—such as warnings on cigarette packages and bans on broadcast advertising—have already had significant effects.

In 1835, Alexis de Tocqueville, a French visitor to America, wrote, "In America the passion for physical well-being is general." Today, as then, health and fitness are front-page items. But with the greater scientific and technological resources now available to us, we are in a far stronger position to make good health care available to everyone. And with the greater technological threats to us as we approach the 21st century, the need to do so is more urgent than ever before. Comprehensive information about basic biology, preventive medicine, medical and surgical treatments, and related ethical and public policy issues can help you arm yourself with the knowledge you need to be healthy throughout your life.

FOREWORD

Dale C. Garell, M.D.

Advances in our understanding of health and disease during the 20th century have been truly remarkable. Indeed, it could be argued that modern health care is one of the greatest accomplishments in all of human history. In the early 20th century, improvements in sanitation, water treatment, and sewage disposal reduced death rates and increased longevity. Previously untreatable illnesses can now be managed with antibiotics, immunizations, and modern surgical techniques. Discoveries in the fields of immunology, genetic diagnosis, and organ transplantation are revolutionizing the prevention and treatment of disease. Modern medicine is even making inroads against cancer and heart disease, two of the leading causes of death in the United States.

Although there is much to be proud of, medicine continues to face enormous challenges. Science has vanquished diseases such as smallpox and polio, but new killers, most notably AIDS, confront us. Moreover, we now victimize ourselves with what some have called "diseases of choice," or those brought on by drug and alcohol abuse, bad eating habits, and mismanagement of the stresses and strains of contemporary life. The very technology that is doing so much to prolong life has brought with it previously unimaginable ethical dilemmas related to issues of death and dying. The rising cost of health care is a matter of central concern to us all. And violence in the form of automobile accidents, homicide, and suicide remains the major killer of young adults.

In the past, most people were content to leave health care and medical treatment in the hands of professionals. But since the 1960s, the consumer of medical care—that is, the patient—has assumed an increasingly central role in the management of his or her own health. There has also been a new emphasis placed on prevention: People are recognizing that their own actions can help prevent many of the conditions that have caused death and disease in the past. This accounts for the growing commitment to good nutrition and regular exercise, for the increasing number of people who are choosing not to smoke, and for a new moderation in people's drinking habits.

People want to know more about themselves and their own health. They are curious about their body: its anatomy, physiology, and bio-chemistry. They want to keep up with rapidly evolving medical technologies and procedures. They are willing to educate themselves about common disorders and diseases so that they can be full partners in their own health care.

THE ENCYCLOPEDIA OF HEALTH is designed to provide the basic knowledge that readers will need if they are to take significant responsibility for their own health. It is also meant to serve as a frame of reference for further study and exploration. The encyclopedia is divided into five subsections: The Healthy Body; The Life Cycle; Medical Disorders & Their Treatment; Psychological Disorders & Their Treatment; and Medical Issues. For each topic covered by the encyclopedia, we present the essential facts about the relevant biology; the symptoms, diagnosis, and treatment of common diseases and disorders; and ways in which you can prevent or reduce the severity of health problems when that is possible. The encyclopedia also projects what may lie ahead in the way of future treatment or prevention strategies.

The broad range of topics and issues covered in the encyclopedia reflects that human health encompasses physical, psychological, social, environmental, and spiritual well-being. Just as the mind and the body are inextricably linked, so, too, is the individual an integral part of the wider world that comprises his or her family, society, and environment. To discuss health in its broadest aspect it is necessary to explore the many ways in which it is connected to such fields as law, social science, public policy, economics, and even religion. And so, the encyclopedia is meant to be a bridge between science, medical technology, the world at large, and you. I hope that it will inspire you to pursue in greater depth particular areas of interest and that you will take advantage of the suggestions for further reading and the lists of resources and organizations that can provide additional information.

CHAPTER 1

ARTHRITIS: AN OVERVIEW

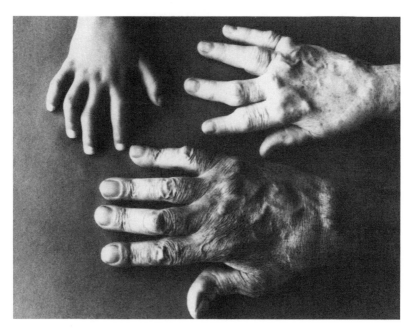

As this photo shows, arthritis affects all age-groups.

Imagine being diagnosed with a painful, often incurable disease that is as old as the dinosaurs, the cause of which is unclear, and the course of which may be marked by anything from occasional discomfort to severe disability. The disease is arthritis, an umbrella term that encompasses almost 125 different disorders with a common symptom—joint pain—to which a wide range of treatments are applied with varying success.

Demography of Arthritis

Sex Differences

	Women	Men
All Types	♀♀ ♂♂	♂ ♂
Degenerative Joint Disease	♀♀ ♂♂	♂ ♂
Rheumatoid Arthritis	♀♀♀ ♂♂♂	♂ ♂
Systemic Lupus Erythematosus	♀♀♀♀♀♀ ♂♂♂♂♂♂	♂ ♂
Progressive Systemic Sclerosis	♀♀♀ ♂♂♂	♂ ♂
Gout	♀ ♂	♀♀♀♀♀♀♀ ♂♂♂♂♂♂♂
Ankylosing Spondylitis	♀ ♂	♀♀♀♀ ♂♂♂♂

For reasons that remain unclear, the prevalence of different forms of arthritis vary according to gender.

Today the Arthritis Foundation estimates that 37 million Americans, or 1 in 7, have some form of arthritis and that the disease affects 1 in 3 American families. The list of arthritis sufferers includes President George Bush, former Chicago Bears linebacker Dick Butkus, former New York Jets quarterback Joe Namath, and actresses Jane Wyman and Annie Potts. The disease has proved to be a particular problem among the elderly. According to the Arthritis Foundation, arthritis strikes almost 50% of those aged 65 or older.

For reasons that remain unclear, gender plays a large role in the disease. Arthritis patients are twice as likely to be women, typically between the ages of 20 and 50, although some forms of the disease, such as *gout* and a spinal arthritis called *ankylosing spondylitis*, are more common in men. The estimated 200,000 children and teenagers with arthritis face their own unique problems.

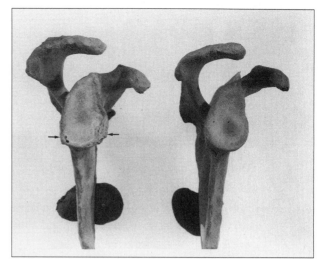

Arthritis is an ancient disease. An arthritic shoulder joint from a prehistoric Alaskan male (left) displays a raised, irregularly shaped rim. A normal shoulder joint is shown on the right.

THE COST OF ARTHRITIS

In 1991 it was expected that arthritis would be diagnosed in 1 million Americans, translating into 1 new case every 33 seconds, and this figure is very likely to grow as the population ages. (It is projected that the number of Americans aged 65 and older will double between 1990 and 2040.) Therefore, it should be no surprise that arthritis is the nation's number one crippling disease.

Arthritis exacts not only a tremendous human toll but a huge financial one as well. Arthritis and related disorders were expected to cost the nation $35 billion in lost wages, medical bills, and related expenses in 1991. By the year 2000, the disorders are expected to add more than $95 billion to the nation's annual health costs, according to the National Arthritis Data Workgroup of the National Institutes of Health (NIH).

Moreover, arthritis already accounts for an annual total of 26 million lost work days and another 500 million restricted work days. It is a major cause of absenteeism in the workplace and of disability payments, too, because more than 7 million Americans are disabled by the condition. Fraud pushes the cost even higher. The Arthritis Foundation estimates that Americans will spend $1 billion on unproven and sometimes dangerous treatments in 1991, amounting to $25 for every $1 devoted to studying the disorder.

ARTHRITIS IN HISTORY

Although arthritis has a profound influence on modern society, its mark was felt in prehistoric times as well. Evidence of *osteoarthritis*, a wear-and-tear form of the disease, is seen in the skeletons of dinosaurs who lived 200 million years ago, and spinal arthritis is evident in the 2-million-year-old bones of ancestral humans. The remains of both Java and Lansing man show that these primitive peoples fell victim to arthritis 500,000 years ago, as did Neanderthal man several thousand centuries later. Scientists have also found arthritis in the bones of

The arthritic spine on this Egyptian mummy is another indication of the disease's existence throughout history.

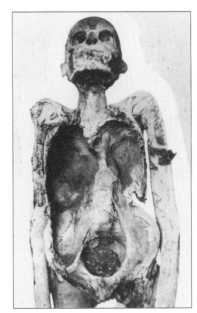

Egyptian mummies dating to 8000 B.C., and *rheumatoid arthritis*, a severe and crippling form of the disease, was making life miserable for the Native Americans who lived in the Tennessee River valley 6,000 years ago. History shows that western civilization has also paid a toll; in a humane gesture the Roman Emperor Diocletian, who began his rule in A.D. 284, exempted the most severely arthritic citizens from taxation.

Early Accounts

The credit for naming and describing arthritis goes to the Father of Medicine, the Greek physician Hippocrates (ca. 460–377 B.C.). In his native tongue the word *arthritis* means "swollen joint," and according to one of his contemporaries, the philosopher Socrates (ca. 469–399 B.C.), it was the most common disease of his day.

Hippocrates also accurately described the condition known as gout. One of the most common forms of arthritis, it usually begins with the

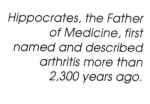

Hippocrates, the Father of Medicine, first named and described arthritis more than 2,300 years ago.

Ancient Rome's extensive system of baths was used not only to promote hygiene but to treat painful joints as well.

painful inflammation of the big toe. For centuries following Hippocrates's observations, all forms of arthritis were assumed to be varieties of gout.

Rheumatism, which is still often used interchangeably with *arthritis*, is derived from the Greek word *rheumatismos*, which means "flowing mucus." The term came about because the Greeks originally blamed the pain of arthritis on mucus flowing from the brain to the joints and throughout the body. (Today the branch of medicine dealing with arthritis and related disorders is called *rheumatology*.)

As centuries passed, differences between various forms of the disease were recognized. For example, the French physician Guillaume de Baillou (1538–1616) was the first to use the term *rheumatism* to describe a problem distinct from gout. By 1907, the newly invented

This 17th-century engraving shows an arthritis sufferer arriving for treatment at a sulfur well in Greece, where the vapors were thought to have medicinal value.

X-ray machine made it possible to distinguish different forms of the disease based on the type of joint damage each of them caused. By 1935, a dozen distinct forms of arthritis had been identified. Over 100 varieties of arthritis are known today.

Early Treatments

The search for a cure, or at least an effective treatment, is undoubtedly as old as the disease itself. Ancient Egyptians tried enemas, and one

Sixteenth-century French physician Guillaume de Baillou was the first to use the word rheumatism *to refer to an arthritic condition distinct from gout.*

Roman physician reportedly treated patients with a shock delivered by an electric eel. In addition, the Romans tried an early form of water therapy, using their extensive system of public baths not only to promote hygiene but to treat painful joints. Centuries later, Europeans attempted to soothe arthritic discomfort through bloodletting, opiates, magnetic jewelry, and electric belts and corsets, showing the difficulty that science has had in dealing with the disease.

One early treatment does survive. In the 18th century, *rheumatic fever*, named for the joint pain it produced, was soothed with a compound isolated from willow bark. Today this medication is known as aspirin, still an important weapon against arthritis.

MODERN INSIGHT

Medical science has made huge strides since the days of Hippocrates, but the causes of arthritis remain only partially understood. Even so,

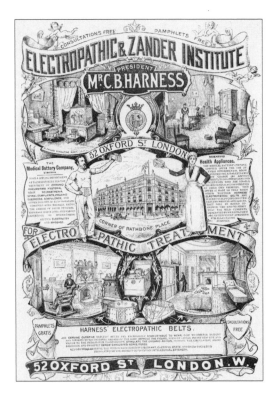

Electric belts and corsets are among the many useless arthritis treatments that have been advertised over the years.

researchers have gained some insight into the sources of this disease, which will be discussed in later chapters. For now the text will look at the factors that do *not* cause arthritis.

Despite countless claims to the contrary, there is no evidence that diet, climate, or stress cause arthritis. Nonetheless, these factors can, in some cases, affect symptoms. Stress can magnify and worsen arthritis pain, and studies have found that a warmer, drier climate may ease symptoms for some rheumatoid arthritis patients.

In the mid- to late 1980s, arthritis specialist Dr. Richard Panush studied the relationship between diet and arthritis. He asked rheumatoid arthritis patients if certain foods made their arthritis worse. Thirty percent of those surveyed believed that some foods did. Panush then tested the link by feeding those foods to patients without telling the patients what they were eating, and he found that only a few people reacted with increased symptoms. Although there is some evidence, in rare instances, of a link between diet and arthritis, the connection still has not been proved. (The exception to this is gout, the dietary aspects of which will be discussed in Chapter 5.)

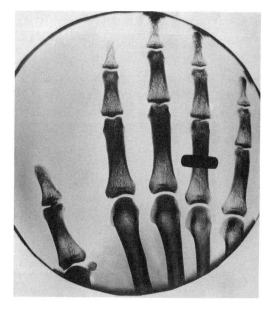

With the development of X-ray machines, doctors were able to distinguish various forms of arthritis based on the type of joint damage they caused.

Bloodletting was another unsuccessful arthritis treatment.

HOPE FOR THE FUTURE

Few forms of arthritis are now curable. Thus, the goal in treating this disease is normally to relieve the symptoms of joint inflammation—pain, swelling, redness, and warmth—and to stop joint deterioration.

Fortunately, new treatments are making relief from these symptoms increasingly possible, and today, patients diagnosed with the disease are less likely to become disabled than were arthritis sufferers of the past. The best news, however, is that the explosion of scientific insight into genetics, the immune system, and the causes of arthritis is leading to safer, more effective treatments. Cures may be waiting in the wings.

CHAPTER 2

OSTEOARTHRITIS

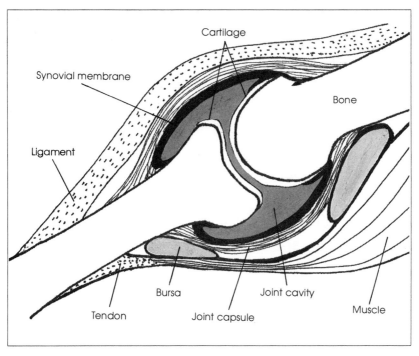

Anatomy of a typical, healthy synovial joint

To understand osteoarthritis, or any form of arthritis, it is necessary to understand its target. This chapter will first discuss *synovial joint* anatomy. (Synovial joints move freely. *Fibrous* and *cartilaginous* joints do not and have been omitted from this text.)

TYPICAL SYNOVIAL JOINT ANATOMY

A healthy joint—the intersection of two bones—is an engineering marvel. Joints are formed in a manner to combine almost effortless mobility with a snug fit. To keep the bones sliding smoothly against each other as the joints twist and turn, and to absorb the shock of activities such as running and jumping, the end of each bone is covered with a smooth, white cushion of *cartilage*. This rubbery material is made up of cartilage cells called *chondrocytes*, strong fibers of the protein *collagen*, and a family of molecules called *proteoglycans*, which combine proteins and a variety of sugars.

Sandwiched between the cartilage on either side of the joint is a thin layer of *synovial fluid*. The name, Greek for "egg white," reflects the consistency of the fluid, which nourishes and lubricates the cartilage. The entire joint is surrounded by the *joint capsule*, which holds the bones on either side of the joint together. The outer layer of the capsule is made up mainly of dense, flexible connective tissue. The inner layer consists of the thin *synovial membrane*, which contains the fluid. The whole package is lashed together and reinforced by tough fibrous *ligaments*, which attach bone to bone, and *tendons*, which attach bone to muscle. A smoothly operating joint also has fluid-filled sacs known as *bursae*. They act as a cushion between bones and tendons or ligaments, reducing friction.

When all of these elements are in place and functioning smoothly, knees bend to jump, fingers caress the piano keys, and a batter swings

Microscopic view of the synovial membrane, which makes up the lining of the joint capsule that holds the bones of the joint together.

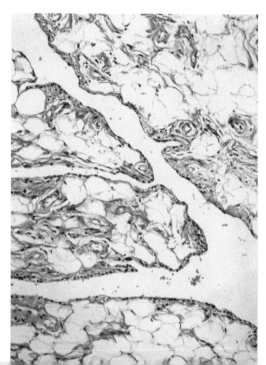

at the pitch. But arthritis can turn that flexible arrangement of fibers, fluid, and cartilage into a rusty hinge.

JOINT DETERIORATION

Osteoarthritis is the most common problem afflicting joints. It is brought on by the wear and tear of normal living, the joint stress that occurs over decades and erodes the cartilage. In addition, research suggests that another factor may contribute to the development of osteoarthritis. Doctors now know that during a person's lifetime special enzymes break down joint cartilage and that the body replaces it with another, less resilient type of cartilage that does not protect the joint

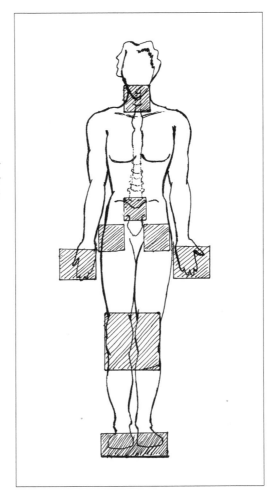

Joints commonly affected by osteoarthritis

as well. It may be that for some reason certain people are more inclined to undergo this breakdown-replacement process, speeding joint deterioration. Injury and infection can also contribute to early cartilage damage.

Regardless of the cause, the result is the same. The normally smooth, spongy cartilage begins to crack and flake, eventually leading to osteoarthritis. According to the National Institutes of Health, an estimated 15.8 million Americans have this condition. For most people with the disease, however, the symptoms are relatively mild. Few osteoarthritis sufferers are affected severely enough to require surgery.

Although symptoms usually do not surface until age 60, deterioration probably begins when a person is in his or her late twenties. By age 40, the joints of most people would, under X ray, show evidence of the disease. A study looking at X rays of hands and feet found some degree of osteoarthritis in 4% of people under 24 years of age.

The disease commonly affects the weight-bearing joints, such as the knees and hips. It also often strikes the spine and fingers. Unlike rheumatoid arthritis, the symptoms of osteoarthritis can be limited to a single joint without affecting the rest of the body.

FACTORS CONTRIBUTING TO OSTEOARTHRITIS

Although osteoarthritis is extremely common, a few factors increase the risk of acquiring the condition. In some cases an individual inherits weak cartilage or is born with a joint misaligned just enough to unnaturally stress the cartilage without affecting how the joint works. Joint injury and overuse can also contribute; for example, construction workers run an increased risk of developing osteoarthritis in their shoulders and elbows, and dancers are more likely to develop it in their ankles and feet. Bricklayers, coal miners, and professional athletes are all at increased risk because they are more likely to injure or put a great deal of stress on their joints.

In addition, joints can apparently receive stress-related damage if an individual is overweight. Researchers who monitored the health of people living in Framingham, Massachusetts, for more than 35 years

Joint injury and overuse can contribute to the development of osteoarthritis. Dancers, for example, are more likely to get the condition in their ankles and feet than are other people.

found a strong correlation in female subjects between being overweight and the development of osteoarthritis of the knee. In fact, weight loss is a standard first step in treating this disease.

The role of exercise-related stress in joint deterioration, however, remains uncertain. Some studies hint that over time certain athletes, including runners, may be more likely to develop osteoarthritis of the knee. But other research, including a study that looked at marathon runners before and after an event, found that the knee joints of runners were typically normal, despite years of running 50 to 100 miles per week.

"We theorize that many marathon runners excel because their knees are well adapted genetically and mechanically to the sport. Individuals whose knees are more susceptible to joint problems may drop out of the sport before they reach the level of these athletes," explained Dr. Frank Shellock of Cedars Sinai Medical Center in Los Angeles, California.

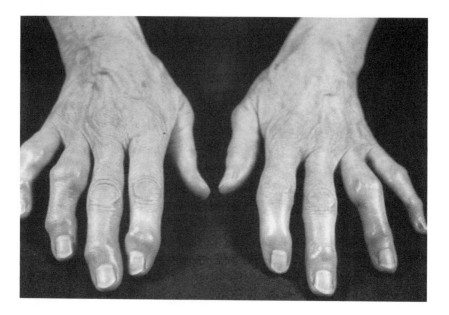

Heberden's nodes, bony growths in the outer finger joints, are often the first symptom of osteoarthritis. The growths in the finger joints below these are called Bouchard's nodes.

Researchers do agree that osteoarthritis sometimes has a family link. *Heberden's nodes*, bony growths in the outer finger joints, are often the first signs of this disease and tend to be hereditary. Appearing years before aches and pains occur, these growths are harmless and are usually left untreated.

In 1990, researchers at Thomas Jefferson University in Philadelphia, Pennsylvania, and Case Western Reserve University in Cleveland, Ohio, reported evidence of an even stronger family link. They studied 19 members in 3 generations of an Ohio family plagued by a severe form of osteoarthritis and managed to pinpoint a genetic mutation. This alteration caused flaws in the production of an important protein in the joint cartilage. That protein, called *collagen II*, is supposed to strengthen the joint cartilage. The genetic alteration was tiny, but the consequences were immense. Family members who inherited the mutation developed the joint pain and stiffness of osteoarthritis when they were in their teens and twenties.

This particular defect is probably responsible for only a fraction of osteoarthritis cases, but scientists are looking for other genetic mutations relating to the disease.

HOW JOINTS DETERIORATE

As mentioned, joints are covered by a cartilage cushion to absorb shock and ease friction. But with age, as the original cartilage wears down and the new, lower quality cartilage replaces it, this protective covering becomes less elastic, provides less cushioning, and leads to more pressure on the underlying bone. The cartilage's smooth, pearly white surface takes on a yellow cast, softens, and begins to flake, resulting in ulcers and cracks.

The flakes can trigger the release of special proteins called *cytokines* by both the cartilage itself and the synovial membrane. In osteoarthritis, the cytokines are suspected of causing further inflammation by prompting the cells in the joint lining and cartilage to produce cartilage-eroding enzymes. It is also suspected that some cytokines

Osteoarthritic joint showing erosion of healthy cartilage

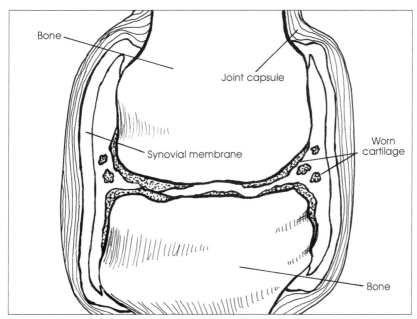

Bone

Joint capsule

Synovial membrane

Worn cartilage

Bone

actually hinder cartilage repair. As the cartilage damage continues, the ligaments lashing the bones together may weaken and contract, causing the joints to become stiff and more difficult to move.

The body does try to fix the damage, but the "repair" can actually make the condition worse. When cartilage erodes, bones apparently remodel themselves into sharp, jagged projections called *bone spurs*. In addition, fluid-filled pouches called *cysts* can form in the bone or close to the joint, causing pain.

SYMPTOMS

No matter where it develops, the symptoms of osteoarthritis are similar and often subtle. They start with a mild, aching soreness, especially when the joint is moved. The pain may come and then disappear for months or even years. Stiffness is another common symptom. In the morning or after periods of inactivity, it will take joints as long as 30 minutes to move smoothly.

As the disease progresses and the joint wears out, pain can be a dull, nagging reminder of the condition, even if a person is reading, watching

An estimated 15.8 million Americans suffer from osteoarthritis. Although symptoms usually do not surface until age 60, joint deterioration can start much earlier.

television, or trying to sleep. Because the individual tends to move the painful afflicted joint less often, the muscles around the joint can gradually weaken from lack of use.

If inflammation sets in, affected joints will become tender and enlarged. In advanced stages, osteoarthritis can drastically limit a joint's normal range of motion, leave joints deformed, and make walking and other activities a painful ordeal.

DIAGNOSIS AND TREATMENT

Osteoarthritis is usually diagnosed through a medical history, an examination of the affected joint, and an X ray. The latter can reveal the damaged cartilage (which appears as a narrowed space between the bones making up the joints) and bone spurs that characterize the disease.

Drug Therapy

Pain is what usually lands people with osteoarthritis in a physician's office. They might be surprised when the doctor prescribes aspirin or a similar mild pain reliever. Inexpensive and effective, these are usually the first step in treating any arthritis. In severe cases, however, inflammation-fighting drugs called *corticosteroids* (laboratory-produced versions of hormones produced by the adrenal glands) may be injected into the affected joints.

Nondrug Therapy

A number of nondrug treatments are available to soothe osteoarthritic joints and protect them from further damage. Exercise is an essential therapy, even in patients with advanced osteoarthritis. The idea is to strengthen the muscles around joints and to preserve as much joint motion as possible. An exercise prescription might include swimming, walking or bicycling. Sometimes exercise is limited to simply moving joints through their complete range of normal motion several times a day.

Participants in an Arthritis Foundation/ YMCA aquatics program; exercise is a useful therapy for osteo- and other forms of arthritis.

Heat treatments involving, for example, a hot pack or warm bath, are also useful, helping to ease pain by relaxing muscles in the area of an affected joint. Cold compresses, on the other hand, can numb a joint area, relieving some discomfort during attacks of pain and inflammation. Arthritic joints can also be protected with the help of splints to immobilize them, or by using canes, walkers, or crutches to take some damaging weight off of them.

If none of the above strategies relieve pain, surgery is another option. This can range from removing the bits of cartilage and bone triggering inflammation to replacing the entire joint. (Artificial joints are discussed in Chapter 3.)

Fortunately for osteoarthritis sufferers, both the medicinal and nondrug treatments for the disease are often quite effective. Moreover, medicine's steadily advancing knowledge of the biomechanics of the disease combined with a better understanding of how to protect and even replace damaged joints are cause for hope for the most seriously affected patients. Researchers are also working to cure osteoarthritis by teaching or tricking the body into making new cartilage. Their work will be discussed in Chapter 7.

CHAPTER 3

RHEUMATOID ARTHRITIS

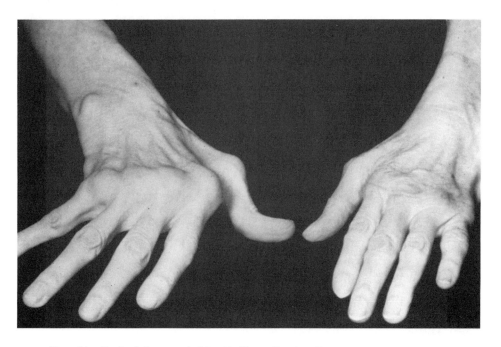

About half of all rheumatoid arthritis patients will develop some disability, and 10% to 15% will have a severe, rapidly progressing form of the disease.

The effects of rheumatoid arthritis are wide-ranging and often severe. Along with joint stiffness and pain (the joints of the hands and feet are usually affected first), symptoms include overwhelming fatigue, weakness, loss of appetite, weight loss, fever, and lethargy. An estimated 2.1 million Americans have the disease, according to the NIH, or nearly 1 in every 100.

Although researchers are gaining greater insight into rheumatoid arthritis, it remains a baffling and frustrating illness for patients and physicians alike. Symptoms can strike suddenly and linger, or they may quickly disappear. Moreover, although surgery, education, and treatment mean fewer patients today face serious handicaps, about half of all rheumatoid patients will develop some disability, and 10% to 15% will develop a severe, rapidly progressing form of the illness. During the disease's earlier stages, there is no accurate method for predicting which patients face the most difficult course. Although symptoms can appear suddenly at any age, the disease commonly strikes individuals between the ages of 20 and 50; for reasons still not known, 75% of those affected are women.

Unlike osteoarthritis, rheumatoid arthritis is an *autoimmune* disease, which means that the body's immune system, designed to fight

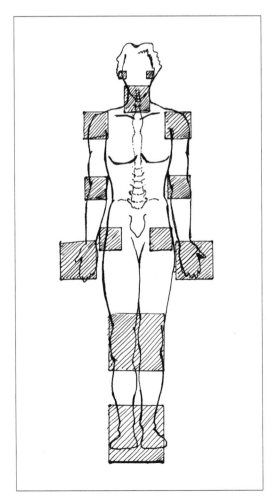

Joints commonly affected by rheumatoid arthritis

disease, actually turns against the body itself and begins to destroy healthy tissue. To understand rheumatoid arthritis, therefore, it is best to know something about how the immune system works.

THE IMMUNE RESPONSE

An infection occurs when a virus or variety of bacteria invades and establishes itself in the body. The result can be severe illness and death, unless the immune system is brought into play to destroy the invader.

The first sign that the immune response has been activated is inflammation, the familiar redness, swelling, and tenderness that develop in an infected area. This occurs because blood vessels at an infection site enlarge, allowing a greater volume of blood to flow to the area. In addition, blood vessels at the site of an infection have a greater tendency to leak, which means that fluid fills the tissue. This fluid contains blood-clotting materials that eventually enclose the infected area within a pouch of connective tissue to help prevent the infection from spreading.

White blood cells are also sent to an infected site to destroy the invading microorganisms or viruses. White blood cells include *neutrophils* and *monocytes*, which are able to push their way through the

White blood cells, seen here in microscopic view, are used by the body to defend against invading organisms. However, they also have a role in the autoimmune response that causes rheumatoid arthritis.

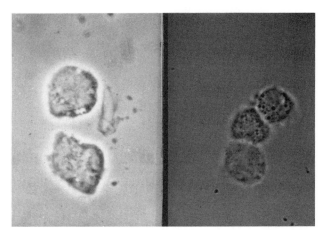

walls of blood vessels and enter infected tissue. Upon arriving at the trouble site, monocytes are transformed into special killing cells called *macrophages*. Both neutrophils and macrophages do their job by engulfing and digesting foreign bodies, which makes them part of a group of cells known as *phagocytes*.

Sometimes that is all it takes to end the infection. But the process often requires a second stage. For this, the body creates cells tailor-made to find and destroy the specific organism or virus that has invaded the body. (The neutrophils and macrophages, on the other hand, will go after any invader.)

The immune system is able to do this because the body can distinguish the materials that make up its own cells and tissues from foreign substances, in viruses or bacteria. The immune system recognizes that a foreign invader contains substances, strange proteins or sugars perhaps, that are unlike the proteins and other large molecules of the body itself. These foreign substances are known as *antigens*. (Actually, the body's own cells also carry antigens, but these are known as *human leukocyte antigens*, or HLAs, and are used by the immune system to help distinguish the body's cells from the invaders.)

During the second stage of the immune response, white blood cells called *B cells* and *T cells* go into action. (B cells and T cells are also known as *lymphocytes*.) They learn to recognize the specific antigen that has been carried in by the invading organism and are programmed to scavenge the body for cells containing that antigen.

In order to do this, B cells mature into *plasma cells*, which secrete *antibodies*—proteins designed to identify the antigen and destroy the invading microbe or virus. In the case of T cells, the entire cell can act as a weapon, attaching to and destroying the foreign agent or the body cell containing it.

In addition to their jobs as microscopic "hitmen," B and T cells help to regulate the overall immune response. For example, special T cells called *suppressor T cells* inhibit the activity of B cells. Another class of T cells, called *helper T cells*, secrete cytokines, which act here as chemical messengers to stimulate the production of more B cells and *killer T cells* (the ones that actually attack the invading organisms) and to encourage the overall inflammatory response.

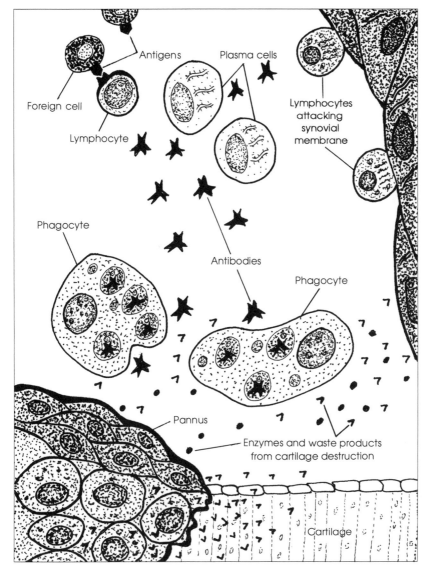

This diagram shows joint damage that results from the autoimmune reaction of rheumatoid arthritis.

Normally, the body's immune reaction and the resulting inflammation end when cells or viruses carrying foreign antigens are destroyed. But in the case of rheumatoid arthritis and other forms of arthritis caused by an autoimmune reaction, the immune system goes on to attack healthy tissue.

Researchers believe genetics and some infectious agent work together to flip the switch. The hypothesis is that due to heredity, some people are more susceptible to developing rheumatoid arthritis. In addition, scientists suggest that an unidentified infection occurs in these people involving an agent with an antigen that is almost identical to one of the body's own HLAs. The immune system, therefore, may be fooled into thinking that normal, healthy cells containing this HLA are actually foreign invaders.

There is some evidence that certain viruses are the foreign agents that help trigger the autoimmune response. Scientists are scrutinizing the rubella and Epstein-Barr viruses, along with the family of viruses that includes the one responsible for acquired immune deficiency syndrome, or AIDS, for their possible role in this reaction. If the agent is identified, and many believe there will be more than one autoimmune trigger, it raises the possibility of developing a vaccine to prevent rheumatoid arthritis.

Left: *T cells and macrophages;* Right: *T cells attacking the synovial membrane*

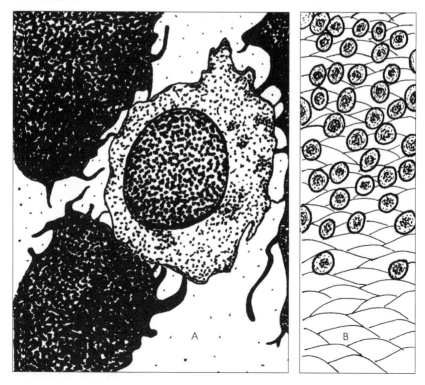

Researchers are also examining the possibility that other factors may help trigger an autoimmune reaction, including diet and on-the-job exposure to chemicals such as carbon, silica, and asbestos. Long-term studies of certain workers, including coal miners and those who have worked with granite or asbestos, found a high incidence of certain types of arthritis, including rheumatoid, among these laborers. One report even indicates a correlation between smoking and rheumatoid arthritis.

An autoimmune reaction begins the way a normal immune response does. Neutrophils and macrophages are marshaled. B cells and T cells are sensitized. But when the antibodies and activated T cells arrive in affected joints problems begin. Along with attacking the foreign invader, the antibodies and T cells react with HLAs in a wide range of normal joint tissue, mistaking healthy cells for infectious agents.

AUTOIMMUNE DAMAGE

In rheumatoid arthritis, autoimmune reactions first target the synovial membrane, causing the normally delicate membrane to thicken and develop folds. Moreover, the white blood cells stimulate the release of the cytokines that, in turn, trigger the production of compounds that actually dissolve cartilage and bone. The body tries to compensate for the damage by forming a *pannus*, which is composed of a combination of connective tissue and the thickened synovial membrane. Ultimately, the pannus can fill the joint, fusing the bones.

Unlike osteoarthritis, the inflammation of rheumatoid arthritis can spread throughout the body. Blood vessels, skin, nerves, muscles, and the heart and lungs can all be affected. Luckily such widespread inflammation is unusual.

ORIGINS OF RHEUMATOID ARTHRITIS

Rheumatoid arthritis was named in 1858 by British physician Sir Alfred Garrod, who recognized it as an ailment distinct from gout and rheumatic fever, which also cause joint pain. His description largely matches the modern definition.

For a long time scientists believed that rheumatoid arthritis was a relatively new disease. Its origins were initially traced to approximately the time of the Industrial Revolution. As recently as the mid-1980s many researchers believed that rheumatoid arthritis did not appear until about 200 years ago.

In 1989, however, anthropologists working in the Tennessee River valley in northwestern Alabama reported evidence of the disease in human remains dating back 6,000 years. They examined more than 20,000 skeletons and found some with joints resembling those seen in modern rheumatoid patients. The skeletons indicated that even in antiquity women were three times more likely than men to develop the disease.

Dr. Bruce Rothschild, director of the Arthritis Center at the Northeast Ohio University College of Medicine, directed the research. He speculated that colonization spread rheumatoid arthritis to Europe and then worldwide.

Healthy finger joints (left) compared to those affected by rheumatoid arthritis

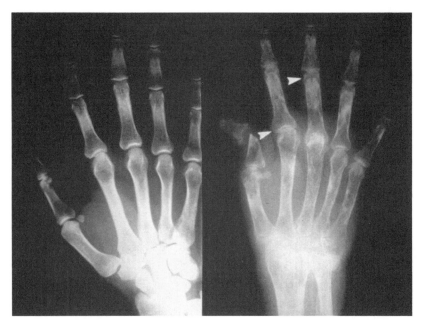

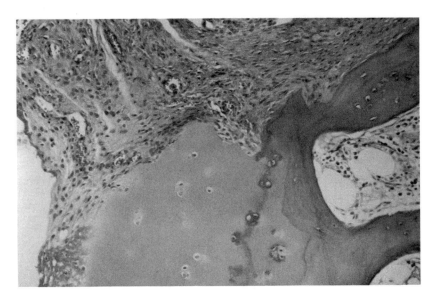

Microscopic view of a pannus; it is formed by the body in response to joint damage caused by rheumatoid arthritis.

"It suggests there was some sort of vector (agent, like a virus or bacterium), something that's transmitted it, that's characteristic of these original areas" where the skeletons were found, he explained. The trigger is thought to be something unique to the site where the disease first developed that could have piggybacked onto the food, wood, and other products shipped from North America to Europe. The debate is not totally academic. Dr. Rothschild noted that pinpointing where the disease originated could help identify the unknown agent that still sets the disease in motion.

The notion that rheumatoid arthritis originated in North America is not universally accepted. Other researchers believe that evidence of the disease exists in the skeletons of Nubian women who lived between A.D. 700 and 1400 in present-day Sudan. Others cite evidence of the rheumatoid features in European bones dating back to before the time of Jesus. Several subjects pictured in paintings attributed to Flemish artist Peter Paul Rubens (1577–1640) suggest that the disease was already present in Europe in the 17th century. Some historians believe that Rubens himself had the disease.

Artificial Joints

According to the National Center for Health Statistics, by the year 1988 there were approximately 1.3 million people in the United States living with artificial joints—including new hips, knees, shoulders, and finger joints. Joint replacement surgery, which exchanges metal and plastic parts for bone, can produce almost miraculous results, restoring mobility and relieving severe pain in patients crippled by arthritis.

The joints most commonly replaced are the hips and the knees. In the former procedure, known as *total hip arthroplasty*, an orthopedic surgeon removes the ball-and-socket joint between the pelvis and the thigh bone, or femur. The artificial replacement, or *prosthesis*, consists of a cup and ball. The thigh portion has a long shaft that is attached to the femur and is topped by a round knob, or ball. The pelvic socket is replaced by the cup.

Left: *X ray of an arthritic knee;* Right: *Patient fitted with an artificial knee*

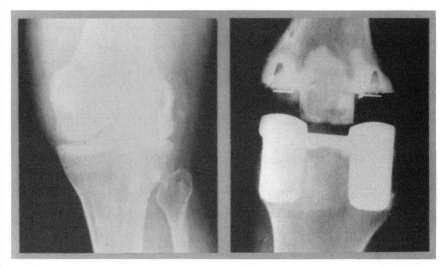

The artificial knee has a different design, featuring a curved piece that attaches to the end of the femur at the knee. It sits in a bottom piece that connects to the tibia, or the shinbone. The femoral section of the knee can then move back and forth like a rocking chair, allowing the leg to bend.

Joint replacement is used after other treatments have not proved satisfactory or when joints have been so damaged by arthritis that any movement is painful. The primary candidates for joint replacement surgery are patients suffering from rheumatoid arthritis or osteoarthritis.

The surgery has drawbacks, however. It is expensive and, like any major operation, it carries the risk of infection, although this is a rare complication. Moreover, although joint replacement allows patients to lead a relatively normal life, the artificial parts do pose limitations. A prosthetic knee, for example, will relieve pain and allow a patient to walk more easily, but it prohibits vigorous exercise on the joint. Similarly, a person with an artificial hip would probably be discouraged from jogging.

The methods of securing artificial joints to the body vary. Traditionally, surgeons have used surgical cement to attach these prostheses to the bones. Yet because the cement eventually breaks down, the new joint can loosen or even slip out of alignment. This means that in general, a new joint lasts only about 15 years. In an effort to solve this problem, surgeons have been studying the effectiveness of artificial joints that require no cement. Such joints have holes in the portion of the prosthesis that fits into the bone. The patient's bone cells grow into the new joint and anchor it. However, recovery from cementless surgery takes longer because patients must protect the prosthesis, and further research will determine how well it ultimately stays in place.

Belgian arthritis expert Dr. Jan DeQueker points to evidence in Italian painter Sandro Botticelli's (1445–1510) Birth of Venus *that may indicate that the 16-year-old model for this work had arthritis. The paintings of Flemish artist Peter Paul Rubens show similar evidence.*

SYMPTOMS AND DIAGNOSIS

The first hint that a person is developing rheumatoid arthritis is often joint pain and stiffness that lingers in the morning or descends after periods of inactivity. This pain can be coupled with fever, weight loss, loss of appetite, fatigue, and anemia. The inflammation can also spread to other joints, typically the small joints of the hands, as well as the elbows, hips, and knees. In addition, a hallmark of the disease is that if a wrist, ankle, or other joint on one side of the body is affected, the corresponding joint on the other side of the body soon will be.

In some cases, inflammation spreads to other parts of the body, including the eyes or the membrane surrounding the lungs. *Rheumatoid nodules* (lumps) often develop at the back of elbows. The nodules usually go untreated because they often appear and disappear on their own and surgery is not a guaranteed cure.

Most patients can look forward to periods of remission during which symptoms ease, followed by renewed pain and stiffness; it is not known why the disease follows this cycle. Disease flare-ups typically begin and end without warning. Rest is often recommended when the disease is most active.

Symptoms and time remain the cornerstones of diagnosis. By definition, a variety of common symptoms ranging from morning stiffness to rheumatoid nodules must be present continuously for at least six weeks before the condition is considered classic rheumatoid arthritis.

Several laboratory tests are also helpful in diagnosing the disease. Ninety percent of rheumatoid patients have a higher-than-normal *erythrocyte sedimentation rate* (ESR), meaning their red blood cells settle to the bottom of a test tube more quickly than normal. However, this test alone cannot be used to make the diagnosis.

Approximately 60% to 70% of patients also have *rheumatoid factor* (RF) in their bloodstream. This abnormal antibody binds to proteins called *immunoglobulins* in a patient's immune system. It is not known, however, whether RF actually plays a role in joint deterioration. As the disease progresses, X rays are useful in identifying joint changes, including narrowing of the space between bones and bone erosion.

TREATMENT

Drug Therapy

Age, occupation, life-style, symptoms, and the severity of the disease all go into choosing a treatment for rheumatoid arthritis. Although there is no cure, treatment is designed to control inflammation and joint destruction, so that arthritic joints can function as well as possible.

Prior to the 1980s, physicians usually tried to treat the early stages of rheumatoid arthritis with drugs—such as aspirin or related medications—designed to control inflammation and prevent other symptoms of the disease. As the inflammation, and thus the joint deterioration, worsened they would gradually introduce stronger drugs designed to

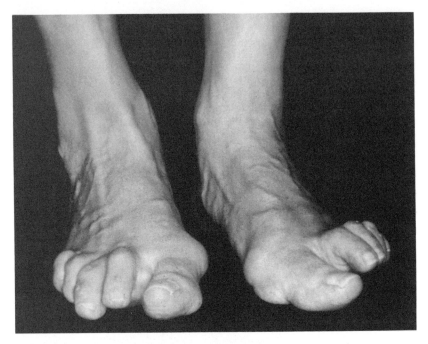

Hammertoe *is a common deformity resulting from rheumatoid arthritis.*

dampen the immune response. But even if the more intense medications worked, by the time they were put to use, a patient had likely already suffered serious joint damage. As a result, during the 1980s doctors began using the immune-system regulating drugs, such as methotrexate, earlier in an effort to protect joints and avert disability.

Unfortunately, current immune-regulating drugs can actually suppress the entire immune system, leaving the patient vulnerable to infection. But researchers are hopeful of finding "magic bullets," medications that would target only specific components of the immune system.

Corticosteroids, the most effective drugs at suppressing inflammation, are also used against the disease but must be administered with care. If taken over a long period of time, they can cause serious side effects, including thinning bones (*osteopenia*), increased susceptibility to infection, cataracts, and diabetes.

Another popular medication for rheumatoid arthritis, one that is still poorly understood by scientists, is the precious metal gold. Injected or taken in pill form, it has been found to curb inflammation and to ease arthritis pain. Unfortunately, gold can cause side effects, including an itchy rash, mouth and vaginal sores, and kidney and bone marrow problems, and it often takes three to four months before the patient notices a benefit from the therapy.

Designing a good treatment plan can be difficult. Dr. Arthur Grayzel of the Arthritis Foundation explained that although current medications offer some relief, they "are less than really effective. They help, but they are not really great. It takes a lot of trial and error with different medications to find one that works in a patient." Chapter 7 will examine some promising leads on improved rheumatoid arthritis treatments.

Nondrug Therapy

In addition to medication, treatment also involves balancing rest with exercise to keep joints flexible and their surrounding muscles strong and to improve overall endurance. When symptoms are severe, stretching exercises to move the joint through its full range of motion are considered sufficient.

"Swan neck" deformity is another effect of rheumatoid arthritis. As the photo on the right shows, the joints lose the ability to bend.

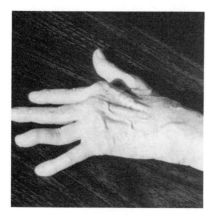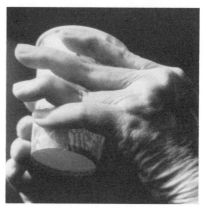

During periods of remission, *isometric exercises* help strengthen muscles. In these, pressure is exerted against an immovable object, such as a wall, so that the muscles contract but the body does not move. Isometrics are recommended because they pit muscle against muscle, making relatively little demand on the joint. To improve overall strength and health, swimming, bicycling, and even walking or climbing stairs are often recommended. In addition, pain relief derived from medication can be supplemented with soothing hot or cold compresses and muscle relaxation techniques. Patients may also wear splints that allow them to rest swollen, painful joints without letting the joints become stiff and bent.

The current treatment approach works for about 85% of patients. The remaining individuals are usually the most severely affected, and some may require surgery to replace a severely damaged and painful joint.

CHAPTER 4

JUVENILE RHEUMATOID ARTHRITIS

An estimated 71,000 children suffer from juvenile rheumatoid arthritis (JRA). This young patient is wearing arm splints to protect her joints.

Youth alone does not guarantee protection from arthritis pain. The Arthritis Foundation estimates that 200,000 American children, some no more than infants, must cope with the disease. Fortunately, the news for these youngsters is not all bad.

The most common form of childhood arthritis—*juvenile rheumatoid arthritis*, or JRA—affects an estimated 71,000 youngsters, according to the foundation. A diagnosis of JRA is applied to anyone 16 and younger with symptoms, including joint swelling, lasting 6 or more weeks. JRA shares some similarities with the adult disease, so it should not be surprising that it also shares the same treatments. Moreover, as with osteo- and rheumatoid arthritis, JRA occurs most often in females, being six times more common in girls than in boys.

Another similarity is that like some forms of adult arthritis, JRA is thought to involve an infection that turns the body's immune system against itself, particularly against the joints.

So far there is no particularly strong family link associated with JRA. Apparently, the brothers and sisters of an arthritis patient normally are at no greater odds of developing the disease than people who come from families in which the condition is not present. Unlike adult

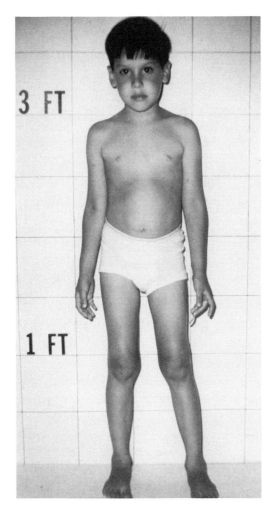

Youngster with JRA of the left knee

arthritis, however, most children outgrow the disease. Only 10% to 20% of patients are left with joint damage severe enough to cause problems later in life, according to Dr. J. Roger Hollister, director of the Rocky Mountain Juvenile Arthritis Center in Denver, Colorado. For most young people, arthritis will just be a memory, and they are only slightly more likely than the general population to develop rheumatoid and other adult forms of the disease later in life.

Although researchers remain uncertain regarding the cause of the disease's disappearance, Dr. Hollister speculates that an essential element is the patient's age. He says that evidence suggests that a child's cartilage is better able to repair itself than an adult's is.

TYPES OF JUVENILE RHEUMATOID ARTHRITIS

Since the 1970s, three forms of JRA have become widely recognized. Before that, the disease was considered to be a mix of aches and pains caused by a strep throat that had developed into rheumatic fever and adult arthritis. Today, juvenile rheumatoid arthritis is generally classified as either *pauciarticular*, *polyarticular*, or *systemic* arthritis.

Pauciarticular Arthritis

The pauciarticular variety is unlike any adult form of arthritis. The name reflects the symptoms. In Greek, *pauci* means "few" and *articular* means "joint." By definition the condition afflicts just a few joints, usually less than five. It seldom affects the same joint on the opposite side of the body.

Pauciarticular arthritis accounts for 20% to 40% of all JRA cases in the United States, estimates the Arthritis Foundation. The outlook for these patients is good; symptoms eventually vanish from 80% of children with the disease, according to Dr. Hollister. Although inflammation continues at first for months, it rarely lasts a year.

In some cases, however, further complications can arise. About one-third of pauciarticular arthritis patients develop *iridocyclitis*, a potentially blinding inflammation of the blood vessels of the *iris*, the colored portion of the eye. The problem is insidious because the eye

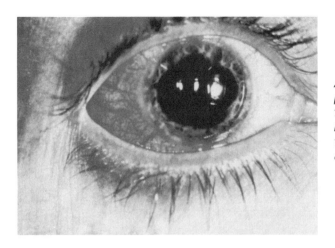

About one-third of patients with pauciarticular arthritis develop iridocyclitis, a potentially blinding eye condition.

does not hurt or change appearance. But if the inflammation continues untreated, vision loss, and even blindness, can result. Often the eye inflammation begins just as the joint inflammation ends. If detected and treated with eye drops containing anti-inflammatory medication, early damage is reversible.

Polyarticular Arthritis

The Arthritis Foundation estimates that polyarticular arthritis accounts for 40% to 50% of all JRA cases. This variety bears some similarities to the adult rheumatoid disease because, like that form, joints become swollen and painful and, if a joint on one side of the body is affected, odds are that the corresponding joint on the other side soon will become inflamed. Moreover, children with polyarticular arthritis often will have rheumatoid factor in their blood.

The weight-bearing joints—hips, knees, ankles, and feet—are common targets of this disease, but often the small joints in the fingers and hands are also attacked. In some cases, it can even affect joints in the jaw or neck. Morning stiffness is often a problem, but hot morning baths can help, and the pain tends to disappear as the day progresses and the child moves through his or her normal routine.

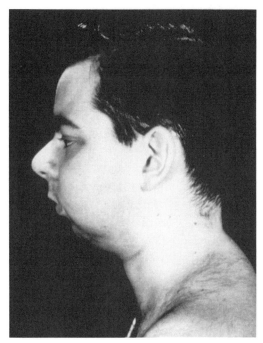

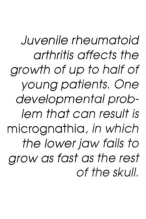

Juvenile rheumatoid arthritis affects the growth of up to half of young patients. One developmental problem that can result is microg28nathia, *in which the lower jaw fails to grow as fast as the rest of the skull.*

Fortunately, most young people with polyarticular arthritis do not face the sort of pain and disability that many adult rheumatoid patients do. In fact, 90% to 95% of children with this disease will enter adulthood with little joint deterioration, according to Dr. Hollister. Only a small percentage experience damage severe enough to require artificial joint replacement. Once again, polyarticular arthritis is most often seen in girls.

Systemic Arthritis

Youngsters with systemic childhood arthritis, also known as *Still's disease*, often face the most difficult course of all JRA patients. "Twenty percent will have a very difficult arthritis," says Dr. Hollister. "These patients account for most of the kids that need joints replaced or have really bad outcomes." Still's can truly be systemic, meaning that it may affect the entire body; symptoms range from fever to swollen lymph nodes to fluid buildup around the heart, chest, or abdomen.

In addition, about 80% of Still's patients have a measleslike rash, but in this case, the small pink dots do not itch or leave scars and do not last long. The rash sometimes comes and goes within a matter of minutes or hours.

The Still's fever is not as benign, however. A child's temperature usually begins climbing at about the same time or times every day, sometimes hovering at about 103 or 104 degrees. This taxes the body, leaving the youngster too spent for much of anything, including school. The fever will come and go, however, with the child's temperature falling back to normal or even dropping below normal later in the day. The exact cause of these fevers is a subject of intense scientific interest.

The anti-inflammatory drugs commonly used to treat the joint pain of Still's disease play a dual role. They are also prescribed around the clock to try to prevent or at least ease the daily fevers. In rare cases, stronger medications, including steroids or immune-dampening drugs

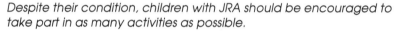

Despite their condition, children with JRA should be encouraged to take part in as many activities as possible.

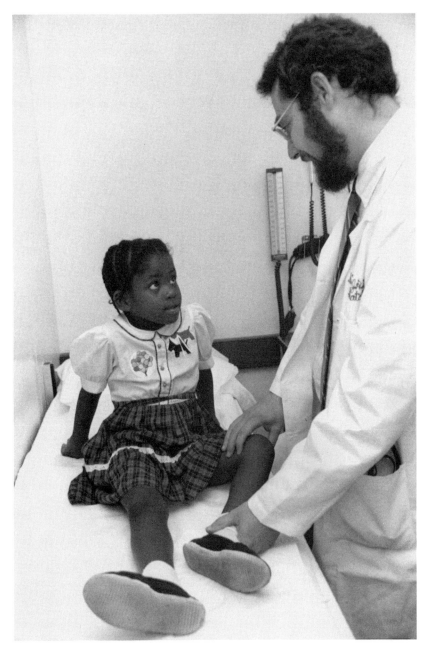

*A specialist at the Hospital for Special Surgery in Manhattan exam-
ines a youngster with JRA.*

such as methotrexate, are used against fevers, but usually the problem will simply stop after a few months.

The joint pain itself is sometimes the last symptom to appear. In rare instances, Still's can cause severe permanent joint damage. The condition accounts for about 20% of all JRA cases, according to the Arthritis Foundation.

ARTHRITIS AND GROWTH

Juvenile rheumatoid arthritis has been found to interfere with the growth of up to half of young patients, according to Dr. Hollister. The youngsters facing the worst growth difficulties are likely to be those with the most hard-to-manage disease. The problem is not completely understood. Scientists are not sure how much should be blamed on the disease and how much on the drugs used to fight arthritis; steroids, for example, are known to stunt growth.

During periods of remission a child can recapture some of the lost growth, but a very small percentage of JRA patients finish their period of natural growth standing less than five feet tall. Researchers are experimenting with a laboratory version of the natural growth hormone in hopes of stimulating growth even during periods of disease activity.

TREATMENT OF JUVENILE
RHEUMATOID ARTHRITIS

Drug Therapy

Aspirin and related drugs are enough to combat pain and inflammation in 60% to 75% of JRA patients. When symptoms prove too much for that approach, gold is often the next option. The treatment helps about 80% of children. Gold is usually given as a weekly injection into a large muscle.

Gold therapy has drawbacks, however. The same side effects facing adult arthritis patients being treated with gold can occur in children. University of Cincinnati researchers reported in a study of 231 Soviet and American children that gold might be safer if taken in pill form rather than by injection. Further studies are underway.

Nondrug Therapy

As with other types of arthritis, exercise is an important part of JRA therapy. In addition, lightweight splints can help hold a JRA patient's arthritic joint in place while the child sleeps, in hopes of easing pain and stiffness in the morning. Heat and cold treatments can also help in the morning or before or immediately after exercise. Sometimes warm wax is used to deliver heat deep into the affected joints of fingers and hands. There is also growing interest in helping children learn to control their arthritis pain by teaching them muscle relaxation techniques; self-hypnosis; and *guided imagery*, in which patients imagine themselves in some restful, soothing environment, such as the seashore

It is important to properly assess a JRA patient's special needs to ensure that he or she receives a proper education, despite the difficulties posed by the disease.

or the mountains. Effective pain control is considered a good measure of how well he or she will do in school and how well the family as a whole will cope with the disease.

Successful treatment involves not only protecting joints but guarding young patients from self-pity and feelings of helplessness, an attitude in which they see themselves as a victim of fate unable to take responsibility for the future. To prevent an arthritic child from being overcome by feelings of self-defeat, doctors believe that parents, siblings, and teachers should have the same expectations of the patient as they do of his or her peers. For example, parents should work with the patient's school to ensure that he or she participates in as many activities there as possible, including physical education. "The mistake most often made is to give in to the limitations which the illness appears to impose," says Dr. Hollister. For arthritic babies, the challenge is to encourage them to use all of their limbs, even ones affected by the disease.

A follow-up study of 100 childhood arthritis patients found that after 25 years, 88 had no signs of the disease. The British researchers reported that 85% of the former patients were employed, married, and self-sufficient.

CHAPTER 5

OTHER COMMON TYPES OF ARTHRITIS

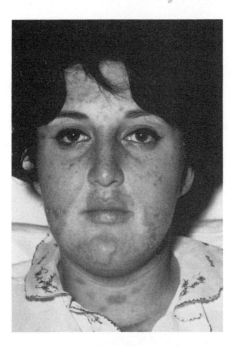

The most common symptom of systemic lupus erythematosus is a facial skin rash. Arthritis is probably the second most common symptom.

In addition to the diseases already discussed, there are other forms of arthritis that afflict millions of Americans. Some, like gout, are well understood and easily treated. Others, such as Lyme disease, highlight the importance of infectious agents such as bacteria in triggering the joint pain and swelling of arthritis. This chapter highlights these and other common forms of arthritis.

SYSTEMIC LUPUS ERYTHEMATOSUS

Systemic lupus erythematosus, or lupus, is a baffling, sometimes deadly autoimmune disorder that can strike the joints. Like rheumatoid arthritis, the underlying cause of lupus may involve an inherited susceptibility (although this is controversial) and an outside agent that turns the body against itself, so that the immune system can no longer distinguish between a virus or strain of bacteria and the body's own healthy tissue. However, the autoimmune reaction that occurs in lupus differs in certain ways from that found in rheumatoid arthritis in that the immune system attacks not only the joints but virtually any organ or system in the body, ranging from the skin or the brain to the heart and the lungs. The effects of this wide path of destruction can be deadly, although, possibly through earlier diagnosis and better treatment, the survival rate for lupus patients has much improved.

Like several other forms of arthritis discussed, lupus occurs most often in women, though scientists are still uncertain as to why. Nine out of 10 patients are women. Black, Hispanic, and certain Native American women are particularly susceptible. All together an estimated 500,000 Americans have lupus.

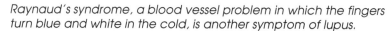

Raynaud's syndrome, a blood vessel problem in which the fingers turn blue and white in the cold, is another symptom of lupus.

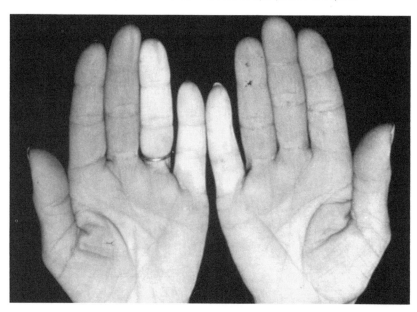

Symptoms

Diagnosing lupus can be difficult. Because the disease can affect almost any part of the body, patients are often told they have anything from rheumatoid arthritis to rheumatic fever.

Lupus is Latin for "wolf," a name derived from the facial skin rash that resembles the mask of a wolf that about half of lupus patients develop. Because of its distinctive shape, this skin condition is also known as a *butterfly rash.*

Arthritis is probably the second most common symptom of lupus. Like rheumatoid arthritis, the pain tends to come and go; it usually strikes several joints simultaneously, favoring the fingers, wrists, elbows, knees, and ankles. However, lupus does not damage the joints. Even after months of joint pain and inflammation, the cartilage emerges unscathed.

The rest of the body is not always as fortunate and may respond with a wide variety of symptoms, including high fever; fatigue; depression; a type of hair loss known as *alopecia*; anemia; mouth ulcers; weight loss; nausea; vomiting; and *Raynaud's syndrome*, a blood vessel problem in which the fingers turn blue and white in the cold.

Diagnosis

Diagnosing lupus usually means looking for a cluster of symptoms—the rash, the arthritis, Raynaud's syndrome, and sometimes protein in the urine (indicating that the kidneys are being affected).

A check for *antinuclear antibodies* (ANA), which react with the nucleus of cells, is also helpful in confirming a diagnosis of lupus. Although it is not known why, almost everyone with active lupus has these antibodies. This factor alone, however, does not automatically mean a person has lupus. ANA is also found in some apparently healthy individuals, in people taking certain medications, and in persons with such long-term infectious diseases as malaria and leprosy.

Given the wide range of potential symptoms, it is not surprising that treatment for lupus varies widely. Patients with mild cases are typically given aspirin or related drugs, or, in some cases, cortico-

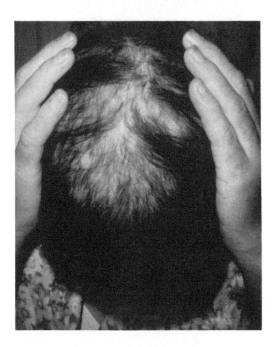

Alopecia, a form of hair loss, can also occur among lupus patients.

steroids. Hydroxychloroquine and other drugs originally developed to combat malaria are also used against lupus. There is no known link between the two disorders, and researchers are not sure why the drugs help, but a 1991 Canadian study demonstrated that patients treated with hydroxychloroquine were less likely than other lupus patients to have flare-ups of the disease.

Flare-ups

Lupus has periods of remission when symptoms almost disappear. When flare-ups occur, they seem to result from "triggers," such as sunlight, infections, injury, and surgery. Some people believe stress and tension can also bring renewed symptoms.

Pregnancy was once thought to worsen the disease, and steroids were prescribed to pregnant patients as a preventive measure. But after following 80 lupus patients through their pregnancies, Dr. Michael Lockshin, in research at New York's Hospital for Special Surgery, found pregnancy really did not effect flare-ups of the condition.

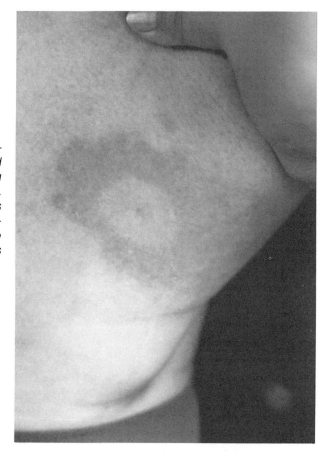

Lyme disease, an infectious ailment spread by ticks, produces a variety of symptoms, the first of which is usually a crimson bull's-eye-shaped rash. The disease also causes joint pain.

The abnormal antibodies associated with lupus do, however, make miscarriages a serious problem for some lupus patients. In addition, one pregnant lupus patient in four gives birth prematurely. Physicians are still looking for ways to protect both the patient and her unborn baby. Often treatment is a combination of aspirin and corticosteroids such as prednisone.

INFECTIOUS ARTHRITIS

Infectious arthritis occurs as a complication of a disease caused by a virus, bacteria, or fungus, or some other type of agent. This can, in a sense, be good news because if the infectious agent can be identified it generally can be eradicated.

Although infectious arthritis accounts for only 1% of all arthritis cases in the United States, it is receiving plenty of attention thanks to the humble tick. Ticks carrying the microbe *Borrelia burgdorferi* have been traced to 46 states and at least 20 countries on 6 continents. This strain of bacteria is responsible for Lyme disease, an ailment with a wide range of symptoms, including arthritis. (The tick species *Ixodes dammini*, *pacificus*, and, possibly, *scapularis* transmit *Borrelia burgdorferi* in the United States.)

The disease is named after the town of Lyme, Connecticut, where it was first described in 1975. That year, worried residents alerted public health officials about the alarming number of local people diagnosed with rheumatoid and juvenile rheumatoid arthritis.

By 1982, researchers knew that bacteria transmitted by the bite of a dark brown tick barely larger than a pinhead were responsible for the joint pain and other symptoms of Lyme disease. The first sign of infection, which develops 2 to 30 days after the tick bite, is usually a crimson, bull's-eye-shaped rash. Symptoms then progress to chills,

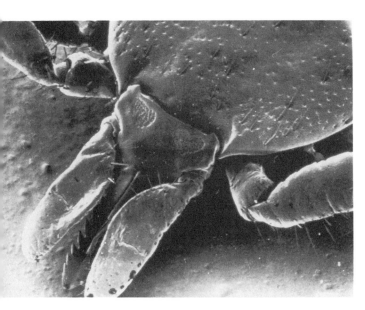

Close-up of Ixodes dammini, *one of the ticks known to carry Lyme disease*

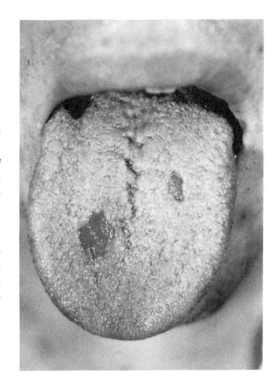

Reiter's syndrome occurs most often in young men and has been linked to sexual transmission and to bacterial infections of the intestine. Symptoms include joint inflammation occurring in large joints or the spine. Another symptom, seen here, is the appearance of lesions in the mouth as well as on the palms, soles of the feet, and, sometimes, the genitalia.

fatigue, painful headaches, and backaches. Signs of the disease sometimes will widen to include heart palpitations, dizziness, or shortness of breath.

Arthritis is usually the third stage, affecting about 60% of untreated Lyme patients, although sometimes not until 2 years after the tick bite. When the joint pain and swelling of arthritis occurs, it usually strikes the knees and lasts for a few days or a few weeks. If identified early, Lyme disease is easily cured with antibiotics. Later in the illness a cure might be more difficult, requiring hospitalization for intravenous administration of antibiotics. Untreated, the disease carries an increasing likelihood of long-term complications. But researchers are still exploring the full extent of the risk.

SPONDYLOARTHROPATHIES

Spondyloarthropathies are forms of arthritis primarily affecting the spine. There are several types of these, including ankylosing spondylitis, *psoriatic arthritis*, *Reiter's syndrome*, and arthritis associated with *chronic inflammatory bowel syndrome*.

Ankylosing Spondylitis

Ankylosing spondylitis is the most common of these disorders and is also the most prevalent form of arthritis in white teenage boys and men. It strikes males more than twice as often as females, beginning as lower back pain that may spread to the hips, knees, and heels. Sometimes ankylosing spondylitis is accompanied by fever, loss of appetite, fatigue, and eye inflammation. In rarer cases, lung and heart problems develop.

Patients are usually between the ages of 16 and 35. One in 100 Americans shows some X-ray evidence of the disease, and the Ankylosing Spondylitis Association estimates that about 500,000 Ameri-

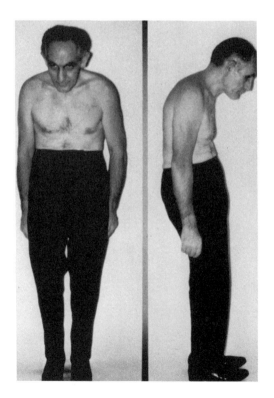

This patient shows the affects of ankylosing spondylitis, an arthritic condition that can leave the spinal column fused and rigid.

cans are affected. The name, which is derived from Greek—*ankylosing* means "stiffening" and *spondyl* means "spine"—describes the problem. If untreated, ankylosing spondylitis can fuse bones in the spinal column and leave the patient with a rigid back.

About 90% of white patients with ankylosing spondylitis have a form of HLA known as HLA-B27. This antigen is also common in the other forms of spondyloarthropathy. But HLA-B27 alone does not cause ankylosing spondylitis. In fact, only about one-fifth of those with the antigen ever develop the disorder. Researchers are looking for the underlying agent that activates the disease.

Growing evidence suggests that various bacterial infections can be the catalyst. For example, researchers have reported a strong immune reaction when tissues bearing HLA-B27 were exposed to antibodies formed against the bacterium *Klebsiella pneumoniae* (which causes a form of pneumonia). This, along with other findings, reinforces earlier studies suggesting that certain bacteria trigger an autoimmune reaction that ultimately causes ankylosing spondylitis. These bacteria contain antigens with similarities to HLA-B27. Scientists speculate that the immune system creates antibodies designed to find and destroy cells containing the bacterial antigens and that, as a result of the likeness between HLA-B27 and the invaders, antibodies may also attack healthy tissue bearing HLA-B27.

A patient being treated for gout. This excruciating condition has been called the "disease of kings and the king of diseases."

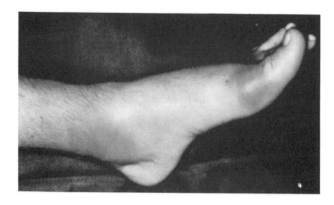

Gout is caused by high levels of uric acid in the blood. Uric acid forms needlelike crystals that are deposited in joints.

While researchers hunt for a cause, many patients spend years seeking a correct diagnosis. The back pain and stiffness that are the first symptoms of ankylosing spondylitis are often blamed on a variety of ailments. But unlike other forms of back pain, ankylosing spondylitis can smolder and progress slowly for decades.

Treatment is usually built around aspirin or related medications and exercise. A few patients require stronger, immune-regulating drugs, such as the aforementioned methotrexate. Sometimes doctors will try steroid injections when other medication fails, and patients occasionally need surgery to replace a damaged joint. Exercise is essential for relieving symptoms and maintaining a flexible back. It can help prevent fusion of the spinal column. Although treatment will not stop the disease, it can provide pain relief and prevent disability. In addition, like many other forms of arthritis, the symptoms can go into remission for long periods before flaring up again.

GOUT

For a form of arthritis that is largely confined to a toe joint, gout holds a very large place in history. Once known as the "disease of kings and the king of diseases," the roll call of gout patients includes Alexander the Great, Louis XIV, Sir Isaac Newton, Martin Luther, John Calvin, Leonardo da Vinci, and Benjamin Franklin.

Today 1 American in 250, or about 1 million people, know the pain of gout. Eighty percent of these patients are men; gout sufferers are

Benjamin Franklin is just one historical figure who suffered from gout. Sir Isaac Newton, Martin Luther, and Leonardo da Vinci are others.

usually in their forties when they experience their first attack. The most common target of the disease is the metatarsophalangeal joint of the big toe.

Gout results from unusually high levels of uric acid in the blood. The uric acid can form needlelike crystals that are deposited in joints, causing inflammation. Some gout patients apparently produce unusually large amounts of uric acid, and there is indication that others have an inherited disorder that leaves their kidneys less efficient in removing the uric acid.

Gout sufferers may also have trouble eliminating substances called *purines* from their body. Since purines are converted into uric acid, eating large amounts of foods rich in purines can, for some people, result in a painful attack. Red meat, alcohol, sweets, and fried foods all contain high quantities of purines.

With its classic symptoms, gout is easy to diagnose. Often there is a triggering event, such as an injury or surgery, or something as simple

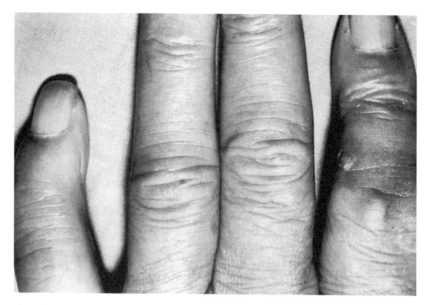

Another symptom of gout is the appearance of uric acid deposits, called tophi, *in the tissues. An ulcerated tophus can be seen on the index finger of this gout patient.*

as eating and drinking too much purine-rich food. Discomfort frequently begins at night, developing into a throbbing, excruciating pain that has been described as being "like the gnawing of a dog." The affected joint becomes hot, swollen, and tender. Examined under a microscope, the needlelike uric acid crystals are visible in joint fluid.

Untreated, an attack can last several days and may never recur. But without treatment the attacks usually do return with increasing severity and can involve other joints of the foot, as well as the ankle, elbow, wrist, and knee.

Fortunately, effective treatments are available for gout. The medication colchicine and *nonsteroidal anti-inflammatory drugs*, or NSAIDs (a group of medications that includes aspirin), are commonly used to control inflammation. After an attack, drugs such as probenecid and sulfinpyrazone that make the body more efficient at eliminating uric acid through the urine are administered in order to prevent another episode. Another medication, allopurinol, is used to decrease the body's production of uric acid.

Gout sufferers are advised to avoid overeating in order to prevent the buildup of purines in the body and are told to drink plenty of water (to encourage urination and, thus, eliminate greater amounts of uric acid from the body).

BURSITIS AND TENDINITIS

Many people suffer unknowingly from arthritis. They may instead call it tennis elbow or turf toe or baseball shoulder, but these are all different types of tendinitis, bursitis, and other conditions related to overuse, injury, or strain of different joint components.

As their names imply, tendinitis is inflammation of the tendons, and bursitis refers to inflammation of the fluid-filled bursae. Treatment usually includes aspirin or related drugs, rest, hot or cold compresses to ease pain, and exercises to stretch the tendons and develop surrounding muscles. Sometimes steroids are injected into the painful joint. Patients usually respond well to treatment, but if not, surgery may be needed to remove inflamed joint components.

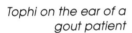

Tophi on the ear of a gout patient

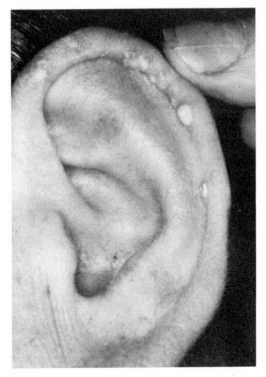

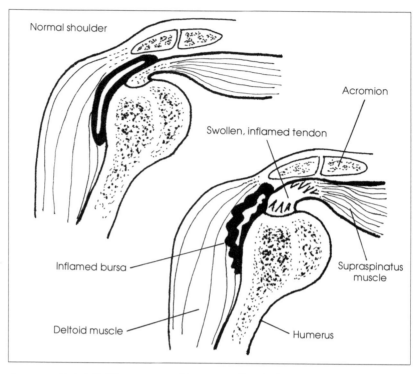

A normal joint (left) compared to one affected by the swelling and inflammation of bursitis and tendinitis.

Treatment may be avoided altogether, however, thanks to research seeking ways to prevent such irritation from occurring in the first place. At Indiana University, Dr. Kenneth Brandt is studying finger techniques used by healthy piano players. With the help of a computerized electronic piano, he is examining the amount of force applied to the fingertips during playing. Dr. Brandt hopes to develop a mathematical model of ideal finger positions so that pianists can reduce the stress on tendons and joints. The same technique might someday help prevent or treat similar problems plaguing others at special risk for tendinitis and bursitis.

CHAPTER 6

ARTHRITIS TREATMENT

British doctor Sir William Osler found treating arthritis patients to be a frustrating task. Medicine has come a long way in the past century, but arthritis remains a challenge for modern physicians.

> When a patient with arthritis walks in the front door, I feel like leaving out the back door.
>
> —Sir William Osler, 19th-century British physician

Sir William would undoubtedly be pleased with today's vastly improved understanding and treatment of arthritis, but faced with the ongoing challenge of helping patients cope on a daily basis, he might still be tempted to slip out the back way. Despite modern advancements, physicians and patients agree that there is still much room for improvement.

MODERN ARTHRITIS CARE

The search for safe, effective arthritis treatments has been dotted with failures and false hopes. For example, in 1936, the steroid hormone cortisone, a corticosteroid, was hailed as an arthritis miracle drug. Then troubling side effects, including weight gain, thin skin, increased blood pressure, brittle bones, and diabetes forced physicians to rethink its usefulness.

Modern medicine's track record regarding arthritis was also marred in 1982 with the introduction of the prescription drug Oraflex. The

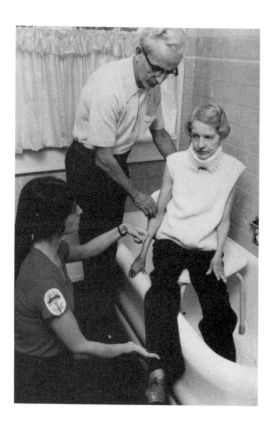

Special devices such as this bathtub bench make daily living easier for some arthritis patients.

drug, which had been approved by the U.S. Food and Drug Administration (FDA) for general use, was withdrawn from the American and international markets by its manufacturer following claims that it had serious and sometimes deadly side effects. The medication was linked to a number of deaths, at least some of them resulting from liver and kidney failure. Despite such difficulties, however, the field of arthritis therapy has seen numerous advances as well.

Around 1940, a physician searching for new tuberculosis (TB) treatments noticed that one subject's arthritis improved in response to the gold the patient had been given as an experimental TB treatment. Today different forms of gold therapy (sometimes it is injected and sometimes it is taken in pill form) are still widely used to treat rheumatoid and some childhood arthritis. Exactly how it works remains a mystery, but physicians believe that gold dampens the runaway immune response that characterizes these forms of the disease.

Over the past 40 years, the explosion of NSAIDs—such as ibuprofen, naproxen, mefenamic, and indomethacin—has also proved a

Nonsteroidal anti-inflammatory drugs—which include aspirin and ibuprofen—are commonly used to treat arthritis pain. The ranks of these medications have grown considerably during the past 40 years.

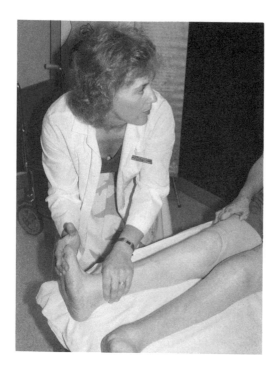

A physical therapist helps an arthritis patient to exercise.

boon for arthritis sufferers. In addition, the ranks of drugs that combat arthritis by regulating the immune system have also grown since the 1960s.

TREATMENT STRATEGIES

The medical treatment of arthritis is increasingly a two-pronged approach. Aspirin and other NSAIDs are the first prong. Gold and medications that dampen the immune system are the other prong. The idea is to relieve symptoms with NSAIDs and use the immune-regulating drugs to slow the joint-damaging disease process, thus preventing disability.

Aspirin

Aspirin was long the foot soldier in the arthritis war. It is inexpensive, widely available, and physicians are familiar with its common side effects. It usually provides pain relief quickly, sometimes within minutes, and can block inflammation if taken in high enough doses.

Aspirin therapy is not without risk, however. Typically a rheumatoid arthritis patient would need 12 to 16 standard aspirin tablets per day, a dose that can cause side effects ranging from ringing in the ears and deafness to nausea, indigestion, and, on rare occasions, bleeding ulcers.

Other NSAIDs

Today physicians normally shy away from prescribing aspirin and treat patients with other NSAIDs, but this is mainly because these alternatives often are more convenient than aspirin, requiring the patient to take only one or two pills daily. Because they can cause the same side effects as aspirin, however, they may be no safer.

The very action that makes aspirin and other NSAIDs risky is also what makes them useful against arthritis. This family of medicines works by suppressing *prostaglandins*, hormonelike molecules secreted by a variety of tissues that heighten pain and fuel inflammation. The problem is that prostaglandins also help protect the stomach lining. Each year, in fact, an estimated 20,000 to 50,000 arthritis patients develop treatment-related intestinal bleeding. Even more troubling, about half the cases are pain free, so the patient may not realize that he

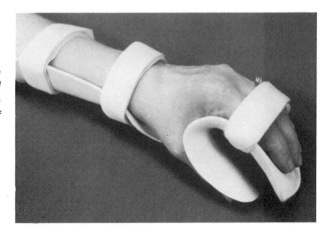

Splints can be used to rest swollen, painful joints without letting the joint become stiff and bent.

or she has a problem. That helps explain why arthritis treatment is linked to as many as 10,000 premature deaths annually.

In 1986, an estimated 100 million prescriptions were written for NSAIDs, and by 1991, there were more than a dozen varieties of these drugs available for use in the United States. Altogether, about 9 million Americans are taking large doses of NSAIDs every day. Ibuprofen, a popular NSAID, can be purchased in both prescription and non-prescription strengths, but most others are available by prescription only.

Other Drugs

The number of immune-regulating drugs being used against arthritis is also growing. They include the anticancer drug methotrexate, drugs used to fight malaria, and a cousin of penicillin called penicillamine. As the 1990s began, arthritis researchers also started to experiment with a therapy that had worked against cancer. This approach involves treating arthritis by combining low doses of several arthritis medications. Because different drugs act on different parts of the immune system, scientists hope that using several at once will be particularly effective against inflammation.

Special devices can help an arthritis patient manipulate doorknobs, handles, and car keys even with stiff, painful fingers.

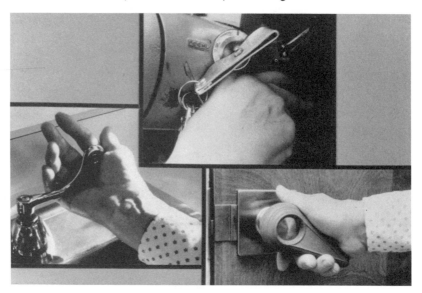

*Arthritis patients exer-
cising to improve
muscle strength*

In 1991, the therapy was receiving mixed reviews. Researchers cautioned that more tests were necessary to judge whether this treatment method would lead to the improvement for arthritis sufferers that it delivered to cancer patients.

Nondrug Therapies

Successful arthritis treatment involves more than just finding the right pill. "The key really is physical activity which provides pain relief and preserves joint function," says Dr. James Fries of the Stanford University Arthritis Center.

An exercise prescription for arthritis patients was once medical heresy. Physicians used to tell recovering heart attack patients to spend the rest of their lives as quietly and sedately as possible, and the same advice was favored for those afflicted with arthritis. No longer—today three types of exercise are usually prescribed for arthritis patients. Gentle exercise is recommended even when the disease is active. The idea is to move an affected joint through its complete range of motion several times daily. Patients are also taught exercises to strengthen the muscles surrounding an arthritic joint and are encouraged to take up an activity such as swimming or bicycle riding designed to improve overall fitness.

The Hands of an Artist

Ann D. Satterfield, who drew a number of diagrams for this text, is well acquainted with the special problems of arthritis. The 33-year-old Manhattan artist has suffered from the disease since childhood.

Although rheumatoid arthritis has affected almost every joint in her body, Satterfield has refused to allow this painful condition to interfere with her career in drawing and sculpture.

She recalls being stricken with juvenile rheumatoid arthritis (see Chapter 4) as a nine year old living in Little Rock, Arkansas. "It happened very suddenly," she says. "The first memory I have of this was getting out of bed in the morning and putting my feet down on the hardwood floor and immediately feeling pain."

Although the disease had already attacked her toe joints, Satterfield paid little attention to the discomfort. As a tomboy, she was used to getting scrapes and bruises. But her parents noticed that she was walking oddly as a result of the pain in her feet. The inflammation soon reached her hands. "And then, very, very quickly after that, my knees were effected," requiring a short stint on crutches, she says.

A seemingly endless series of medical tests confirmed a diag-

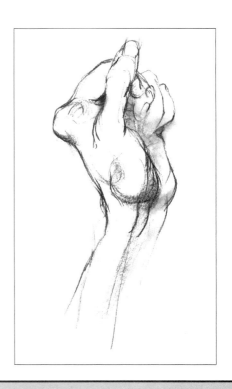

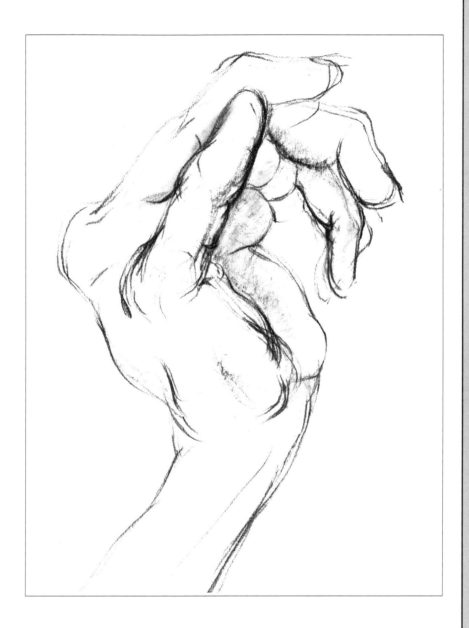

nosis of arthritis, and in a short time Satterfield's life was very much changed. A youngster who had once passed the time rough-housing with other neighborhood kids suddenly found it painful just to pull on her clothes in the morning. "I had to move slower. I got impatient with myself a lot," she says. "A lot of family members and friends got impatient with me, too, because they weren't used to seeing me go through that."

"I was really angry because I couldn't enjoy playing with other kids my own age," explains Satterfield. "And so I immediately felt isolated." To make matters worse, her parents and physicians—perhaps trying to minimize a difficult situation—seemed reluctant to talk with her about the psychological cost of the disease. In retrospect, Satterfield realizes, "It's important to be able to understand what happens to the patient emotionally."

Even so, Satterfield refused to allow arthritis to hamper her career. "I've been an artist all my life," she says. "Even before I had arthritis I would spend hours and hours drawing and writing stories and illustrating them. . . . I always loved making things. And when I got arthritis, it never occurred to me not to do that."

She went on to major in sculpture and photography at Washington University in St. Louis, Missouri, and later received a graduate degree in fine arts from a school in Rochester, New York. Despite her condition, she did not shy away from sculpting in steel or marble, holding heavy objects in the crooks of her elbows, or asking fellow students to help her in the studio. "I let my ideas guide me rather than the arthritis," she says.

These days Satterfield is a professional illustrator, but works in many other artistic mediums, despite the inevitable toll her vocation takes on her inflamed joints. Although Satterfield has not been limited by arthritis, the disease has influenced her art. As the illustrations on pages 80–81 suggest, arthritis is one of the themes she incorporates into her work. In this case she has drawn her own arthritic joints. "Drawing myself is another way to know myself," she says. "And it's another way to look within."

Heat and cold are often used for pain relief. These treatments can be as simple as applying an ice pack or soaking in a warm bath. Sometimes using a flexible splint to rest and protect a joint is essential to pain control during a disease flare-up. Another type of treatment, *ultrasound therapy*, relies on sound waves to ease pain by increasing blood flow and warming muscles.

Preventive steps against arthritis include maintaining a normal weight and protecting one's joints through good posture, as well as a common-sense approach to exercise.

Patient Education

Patient education can help relieve pain and protect against the depression a debilitating illness can cause. This strategy involves more than just explaining the how and why of the disease. Ideally it includes

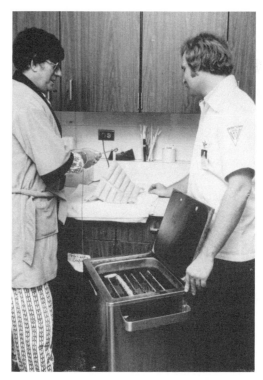

A physical therapist teaches an arthritis patient how to prepare a heat pack. Patient education is essential in helping individuals deal with their disease.

teaching patients how to cope with the pain, disability, and anxiety associated with a chronic disease.

One aspect of an arthritis patient's education might involve instruction in muscle relaxation techniques and self-massage. But education can go much deeper than that. "What we try and do is teach people a systematic method to cope with problems, a way to conceptualize the problem in terms of behavior," explains Dr. Laurence Bradley of the University of Alabama at Birmingham. In other words, if an arthritis patient complains of feeling depressed, Dr. Bradley would suggest that this person review his or her behavior to see if it is contributing to the unhappy mood. The patient might, for example, be staying in bed too long or avoiding exercise.

Depression is a common side effect of any chronic, painful disease such as arthritis. Dr. Bradley estimates that 20% of chronic pain patients, regardless of the pain's source, are also battling a major depression. Along with physical discomfort, arthritis patients sometimes must adjust to physical changes that can leave them feeling less attractive, more limited in their activities, and sometimes earning less money.

Growing evidence shows, however, that with education and support, patients can adjust. A 1988 study at the Bowman Gray School

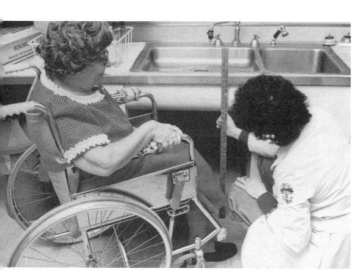

A therapist can help assess whether an arthritis patient will be able to live independently at home.

of Medicine at Wake Forest University in Winston-Salem, North Carolina, found that a year after completing a self-help program, rheumatoid arthritis patients still reported less pain and anxiety and greater activity than arthritis patients who did not receive the training. The program included relaxation training, goal setting, and discussions of different strategies for coping.

This device was advertised as a cure for a number of unrelated conditions, including arthritis. Today quack arthritis cures attract $1 billion annually.

Quack and Unproven Cures

Arthritis quackery and fraud have, unfortunately, kept pace with legitimate medical advances. As far back as the 1850s, more than 1,500 purported cures were available to any American with the money to buy them. The main ingredients then were often flavored water, alcohol, narcotics, and outright poisons.

Today's "miracle" arthritis cures—which attract $1 billion annually—would look familiar to earlier hustlers. These treatments often involve special diets or diet supplements and devices such as copper bracelets or radioactive gadgets. As in the past, peddlers usually promise relief not only from many different forms of arthritis but from other conditions as well, including diabetes and baldness. For example, the Energy Point Stimulator, was sold in the 1980s to provide relief from arthritis, migraines, and indigestion. Buyers were instructed to use this 20th-century magic wand to deliver a curative electric charge to certain "energy points" in the ear. In 1988, a court order issued in Kansas allowed the FDA to destroy several shipments of the wands.

Useless diet suggestions have included dosing oneself with cod liver oil to lubricate the joints, ingesting blackstrap molasses or alfalfa, or consuming endless herbal combinations. Arthritis patients can also

The foam bath was another attempt to treat arthritis.

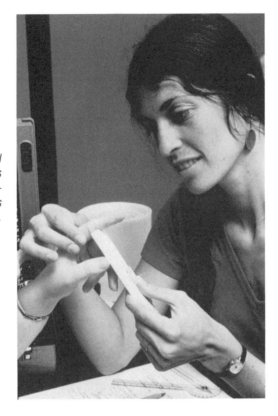

An occupational therapist evaluates the amount of swelling in an arthritis patient's joints.

pay for the privilege of sitting in an abandoned mine to absorb radon—given off by the disintegration of naturally occurring uranium—even though radiation has not been found to provide long-term arthritis relief and doctors say there is no proof that the mines can offer any real benefit.

Another unproven treatment, the drug dimethyl sulfoxide (DMSO) has more lives than a cat. Although the FDA has approved it only for use against an uncommon bladder disorder known as interstitial cystitis, desperate arthritis patients have been trying DMSO since the 1960s. It may provide minor pain relief, but there is no demonstrated long-term benefit associated with using DMSO. Since it is often available in strengths designed for veterinary use, DMSO can also cause nausea, headaches, and skin rashes.

Along the U.S.-Mexico border arthritis is a growth industry. The border is home to a variety of arthritis clinics often peddling mysterious pills billed as miracle drugs from Europe. The clinics and their treatments have proven harmful, even deadly on occasion.

Why do so many arthritis sufferers fall prey to medical quackery? A 1986 FDA survey may provide part of the answer. In the study, which looked at 247 arthritis patients, 18% reported they almost always had a significant amount of pain, and 22% said their arthritis frequently caused significant pain. About one in three said they would try anything to improve their arthritis, even if it sounded silly or had a small likelihood of success.

In addition, because arthritis is often a cyclic disease, with pain coming and going at intervals, odds are that a patient's condition will improve after a while. As a result, some quack treatments are perceived as being effective when they are not. Moreover, a patient eager for help may experience a *placebo effect* from an unproven therapy. That is, the individual may temporarily feel better after the treatment simply because he or she expects the therapy to work, not because the treatment itself was valuable.

CHAPTER 7

ARTHRITIS RESEARCH

Arthritis researchers discuss their work.

After centuries of suffering, arthritis patients have never faced a brighter future. In the 1980s, lupus survival rates rose dramatically, and scientists identified the cause and treatment of Lyme disease as well as the genetic mutation responsible for some osteoarthritis. In addition, researchers have found a way to produce ankylosing spondylitis in rats, a development that should speed research into the cause of this condition, thus leading to better treatment and possibly a cure. By 1990 more than 200 new arthritis drugs were awaiting federal approval.

There has also been an explosion of basic knowledge about human heredity, and it is expected that in the 21st century, arthritis patients will benefit tremendously from research begun in the mid-1970s in hopes of answering basic questions about how the immune system functions. Arthritis treatment is also benefiting from projects undertaken to deal with a broad range of other human ailments, including the immune system studies conducted by AIDS researchers. Moreover, there is an international effort to decode all the genes in the human body. The 15-year-long Human Genome Project, which officially began in 1990, should allow scientists to find the genetic mutations linked to arthritis.

Researchers are predicting a future of more specific and less toxic treatments, a future in which it is possible to prevent some forms of arthritis with vaccines and to reverse others.

SOLVING A GENETIC PUZZLE

Understanding the underlying cause of different forms of arthritis may one day help scientists prevent the disease. With that as a goal,

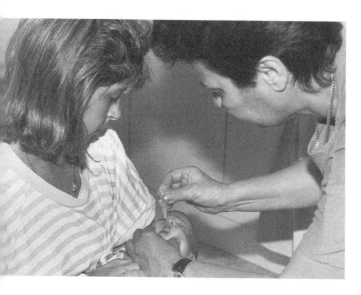

An infant is vaccinated against polio. Researchers predict that one day, vaccines against arthritis will be available.

researchers are working to understand exactly how people inherit a tendency to develop certain forms of arthritis.

"One lucky break would allow people to unravel the whole process," said Dr. Grayzel of the Arthritis Foundation. Indeed there is a rapidly growing list of diseases in which the basic genetic mutation is known. Such ailments include cystic fibrosis, Duchenne muscular dystrophy, and cancers of the lung, breast, and colon. Pinpointing the genes responsible for arthritis holds the potential of one day replacing those genes, a sophisticated form of therapy that is already being used experimentally to treat cancer and a rare inherited immune defect.

EXAMINING OTHER FACTORS

Along with the bacteria and viruses already linked to arthritis, other agents implicated in the disease include parasites, carbon, silica, and

Scientists from the National Institutes of Health discuss an experimental genetic treatment used on a four-year-old girl with an immune system disorder. Gene therapy may also one day be used to treat forms of arthritis that have a hereditary component.

Researchers involved in the Human Genome Project can store and analyze information via computer. The project, in which researchers plan to map every gene in the human body, should allow scientists to find genetic mutations linked to arthritis.

asbestos. According to Dr. Derrick Brewerton in the rheumatology department of Westminster Hospital in London, England, the agents responsible for triggering the disease may vary from person to person as well as from one type of arthritis to another. The responsible trigger might also differ with each disease flare-up.

Evidence also shows that the central nervous system plays a role in arthritis. Physicians have known for a long time that when arthritis occurs in someone who survived a stroke or some other central nervous system (CNS) trauma, the arthritis spares joints on the side of the body affected by the damage. In rats, scientists can delay or diminish the severity of arthritis by cutting the sciatic nerve.

In addition, animal studies suggest that interaction between different components of the nervous system contribute to arthritic damage. Such research holds the promise that one day scientists will develop a whole new class of drugs that use the nervous system to combat arthritis.

Federal researchers also reported evidence of a defect in production of corticosteroids in the brains of arthritic rats. Drs. Ronald Wilder and Esther Sternberg of the National Institute of Arthritis and Musculoskeletal and Skin Diseases found that the hypothalamus in the brain of affected rats was unable to produce enough of these hormones, which are crucial to regulating inflammation.

Researchers at the University of California at San Francisco and Boston's Massachusetts General Hospital are interested in whether *substance P*, one of a group of molecules known as *peptides*, plays a role in inflammation. Substance P is already believed to aid in transmitting pain impulses to the brain, and the scientists have demonstrated that destroying nerves containing substance P does weaken the body's immune response.

The researchers also reported differences in concentrations of the substance in joints. For example, larger amounts of the peptide are found in the ankle than the knee, and they also found that certain nerve cells that react only to intense, potentially harmful stimulation are more common in the ankle than the knee. The scientists speculate that both the peptide and the nerve cells might help explain why arthritis is more likely to develop in the ankle than the knee. The work also suggests that reducing levels of substance P might ease the condition.

ON THE HORIZON

Researchers and pharmaceutical companies expect a new generation of arthritis medications to work by interrupting the inflammatory cycle. To do so, such medicines would act on the immune cells involved. Drs. Kathryn Sewell and David Trentham of Harvard Medical School and Beth Israel Hospital reported promising early results with that approach. They treated 13 rheumatoid arthritis patients using a specially engineered human protein carrying a poison. The protein was designed to bind with T cells, in order to halt arthritis inflammation. Twelve of the 13 patients improved after a week of treatment with the toxin. Side effects included mild nausea and a slight fever.

Another treatment approach being studied involves using a laboratory version of a natural protein that blocks the action of the cytokine *interleukin-1* (IL-1). The protein is called *interleukin-1 receptor antagonist*, or IL-1ra, and has been found, in animals, to block inflammation and bone destruction. Scientists believe that it is normally produced in small amounts and stops inflammation by interfering with the action of IL-1. Researchers are also working on a drug that attracts and soaks up IL-1 like a sponge. Other companies are studying compounds that block IL-1 production entirely.

"The whole idea is that you move from a shotgun approach to more selective treatment," explained Dr. Arnold Postlethwaite, a University of Tennessee arthritis researcher. Dr. Grayzel of the Arthritis Foundation predicted it would be the year 2000 before such biological agents were widely available.

Meanwhile, work continues on unraveling the mysteries of the entire immune mechanism in hopes of finding new ways to treat,

An arthritis patient playing the piano; with proper care, arthritis does not have to mean the end of a full life.

monitor, or prevent arthritis. After studying the cytokine interleukin-6 (IL-6), Dr. Martin Lotz of the Scripps Clinic and Research Foundation in La Jolla, California, concluded that it could play a major role in inflammatory arthritis. The finding suggests another possible path for blocking damaging inflammation.

Inflammation does not play a central role in osteoarthritis, so investigators are banking on other novel approaches to treat this disease. Promising research indicates that it may be possible to spur the body to replace damaged cartilage in an osteoarthritic joint with a variety that is of higher quality than the normal replacement material. Dr. Daniel Grande at North Shore University Hospital in Manhasset, New York, actually repaired cartilage in the knees of rabbits using a fairly resilient tissue grown from chondrocytes tended in the laboratory.

Other researchers are experimenting with ways of growing cartilage in the laboratory using a sort of frame made from a derivative of collagen. Dr. Kevin Stone, a San Francisco, California, orthopedic surgeon, has studied this approach in dogs. He removed cartilage cushioning the dog's knee and cut holes in this cartilage, plugging them with the collagen-based frame. He found that, under the right conditions, new cartilage would grow around the frame. When transplanted back into the dogs, the results were promising. A year after transplant, the frame was absorbed and healthy cartilage provided needed protection.

Dr. Rose Fice of the Indiana University School of Medicine suggests that another treatment approach might be to transfer healthy cartilage from one joint in the patient's body to replace damaged cartilage in another joint. Researchers are also looking into the possibility of transplanting cartilage from a deceased donor to an osteoarthritis patient.

CONCLUSION

Countless questions still remain for arthritis researchers and generations of patients to come. Before physicians can hope to prevent or cure joint disease, they will have to unlock its source. What ignites the autoimmune response? Is a virus the trigger? What role does heredity play?

Chances are that future studies such as the Human Genome Project will help answer many of these questions. Certainly, considering the vast human and financial toll that arthritis takes, society has a great deal to gain from safer, more effective treatments for this very old and puzzling disease.

APPENDIX:
FOR MORE INFORMATION

The following is a list of organizations in the United States and Canada that can provide further information about arthritis and related disorders.

GENERAL INFORMATION

American College of Rheumatology
60 Executive Park Drive South
Suite 150
Atlanta, GA 30329
(404) 633-3777

Arthritis Foundation
1314 Spring Street, NW
Atlanta, GA 30309
(404) 872-7100 (in Atlanta)
(800) 283-7800 (outside Atlanta)

Arthritis Society
250 Bloor Street East
Suite 401
Toronto, ON M4W 3P2
Canada
(416) 967-1414

The Health Education Center
1080 Lexington Avenue
New York, NY 10021
(212) 439-2980

National Arthritis and Musculoskeletal
and Skin Diseases Information
Clearinghouse
Box AMS
9000 Rockville Pike
Bethesda, MD 20892
(301) 495-4484

The National Institute of Arthritis and
Musculoskeletal and Skin Diseases
9000 Rockville Pike
Building 31, Room 4C32
Bethesda, MD 20892
(301) 496-4353

Rheumatoid Disease Foundation
5106 Old Harding Road
Franklin, TN 37064

ANKYLOSING SPONDYLITIS

Ankylosing Spondylitis Association
P.O. Box 5872
Sherman Oaks, CA 91413
(800) 777-8189

LYME DISEASE

Lyme Borreliosis Foundation, Inc.
National Headquarters
P.O. Box 462
Tolland, CT 06084
(203) 871-2900

SYSTEMIC LUPUS
ERYTHEMATOSUS

The American Lupus Society
(213) 542-8891

Lupus Erythematosus Society of Alberta
P.O. Box 8154, Station "F"
Calgary, Alberta T2J 2V3

Canada
(403) 233-8696

The Lupus Foundation of America
(800) 558-0121

Lupus Network
(203) 372-5795

National Jewish Center
  for Immunology and
  Respiratory Medicine
1400 Jackson Street
Denver, CO 80206
(303) 355-5864 (in Denver)
(800) 222-LUNG (outside Denver)

FURTHER READING

Ahmed, Paul I., ed. *Coping with Arthritis*. Springfield, IL: Thomas, 1988.

Aladjem, Henrietta. *Understanding Lupus: What It Is, How to Treat It, How to Cope with It*. New York: Scribners, 1986.

Arthritis Foundation. *Arthritis: Basic Facts*. Atlanta: Arthritis Foundation, N. d.

Arthritis Foundation. *Arthritis Information: Exercise and Your Arthritis*. Atlanta: Arthritis Foundation, 1986.

Arthritis Foundation. *Arthritis Information: Osteoarthritis*. Atlanta: Arthritis Foundation, 1990.

Arthritis Foundation. *Arthritis: Unproven Remedies*. Atlanta: Arthritis Foundation, 1987.

Arthritis Foundation. *Medical Information Series: Rhuematoid Arthritis*. Atlanta: Arthritis Foundation, 1983.

Arthritis Foundation and Arthritis Health Professions Association. *Overcoming Rheumatoid Arthritis: What You Can Do for Yourself*. Atlanta: Arthritis Foundation and Arthritis Health Professions Association, N. d.

Arthritis Foundation Editors. *Understanding Arthritis: What It Is, How It's Treated, How to Cope with It*. New York: Scribners, 1985.

Barrett, Stephen. *Health Schemes, Scams and Frauds.* New York: Consumer Reports Books, 1990.

Decker, John, ed. *The Reliable Healthcare Companion: Understanding and Managing Arthritis.* New York: Avon Books, 1987.

Fernandez-Madrid, Felix. *Treating Arthritis: Medicine, Myth, and Magic.* New York: Plenum, 1989.

Fries, James F. *Arthritis: A Comprehensive Guide.* Reading, MA: Addison-Welsey, 1990.

Habicht, Gail, Gregory Beck, and Jorge Benach. "Lyme Disease." *Scientific American* 257 (July 1987): 78.

Jarvis, D. C. *Arthritis and Folk Medicine.* New York: Fawcett Books, 1985.

Lenox Hill Hospital. *Bursitis.* New York: Lenox Hill Hospital, 1990.

Lenox Hill Hospital. *Osteoarthritis: A Special Concern in Later Life.* New York: Lenox Hill Hospital, 1990.

Lorig, Kate, and James F. Fries. *The Arthritis Help Book.* Reading, MA: Addison-Wesley, 1990.

Moskowitz, Roland W., and Marie R. Haug. *Arthritis and the Elderly.* New York: Springer-Verlag, 1985.

Moskowitz, Roland W., et al. *Osteoarthritis: Diagnosis and Management.* Philadelphia: Saunders, 1984.

Pfizer Central Research. *Lyme Disease.* Groton, CT: Pfizer Central Research, 1990.

Philips, Robert H. *Coping with Osteoarthritis: A Guide to Living with Arthritis for You and Your Family.* Garden City Park, NY: Avery, 1989.

Robinson, Harold S., ed. *You Asked About Rheumatoid Arthritis: Reassuring Advice from a Distinguished Medical Team for All Who Suffer from North America's No. 1 Crippling Disease.* New York: Beaufort Books, 1982.

Scott, J. T. *Arthritis and Rheumatism: The Facts.* New York: Oxford University Press, 1980.

Spencer, Toni. *Arthritis Self-preservation: Arthritis Can't Make Me Cry.* Tulsa, OK: Jigsaw, 1989.

Williams, Gordon F. *Children with Chronic Arthritis: A Primer for Patients and Parents.* Littleton, MA: PSG, 1981.

GLOSSARY

ankylosing spondylitis the most common form of spondyloarthropathy, characterized by lower back pain that spreads to the hips, knees, and heels and may be accompanied by fever, loss of appetite, and lung and heart problems; possibly caused by bacterial infections; if untreated, can result in fused bones in the spinal column and a rigid back

antibodies protein substances that are developed to interact with and destroy cells or microbes (microorganisms) containing antigens

antigens foreign substances in the body composed of matter that is not part of the body itself; antigens induce the formation of antibodies

antinuclear antibodies ANA; antibodies that react with the nucleus of a cell; may be found in people with lupus

arthritis Greek for "swollen joint"; inflammation of a joint or joints, usually accompanied by pain and changes in the structure of the afflicted body part

autoimmune disease a disease in which the immune system turns against the body and produces antibodies that destroy healthy tissue

bursae fluid-filled sacs that reduce friction between bones and tendons or ligaments

bursitis an inflammation of the bursae

cartilage the rubbery material found at the end of each bone that absorbs shock and allows the bones to move smoothly; composed of chondrocytes, collagen, and proteoglycans

collagen the white, fibrous, insoluble protein that provides the framework for skin, tendons, bones, cartilage, and all other connective tissue

corticosteroids hormones produced in the cortex of the adrenal glands; also, drug versions used to reduce arthritis inflammation

gout an acute form of arthritis beginning in the joints of the knee or foot and resulting from excess levels of uric acid in the blood

Heberden's nodes bony growths in the upper finger joints that usually appear years before the outbreak of osteoarthritis

human leukocyte antigens proteins used by the immune system to distinguish its own tissue from foreign invaders

iridocyclitis an inflammation of the blood vessels in the iris that can cause blindness but is treatable with anti-inflammatory medication if detected in its early stages; a possible side-effect of pauciarticular arthritis

isometric exercises exercises in which pressure is exerted against an immovable object, thus building up muscles while keeping joints stationary; ideal for arthritis patients in remission

ligaments bands of strong fibrous connective tissue that bind bones together

lupus systemic lupus erythematosus; an autoimmune disease that can affect any organ or system in the body; symptoms include a facial skin rash, arthritis that strikes several joints at once but does not damage the cartilage, high fever, depression, and weight loss

Lyme disease an infectious disease contracted by a bite from a tick carrying the bacteria *Borrelia burgdorferi*; symptoms include rash, chills, fatigue, painful headaches, backaches, and arthritis

osteoarthritis the most common type of arthritis, in which normally spongy cartilage cracks and flakes; women who are overweight or people who overuse certain joints are more susceptible to osteoarthritis

pannus a tissue spreading from the synovial membrane and connective tissue that can fill joints and fuse the surrounding bones; occurs in rheumatoid arthritis

pauciarticular arthritis a type of childhood arthritis affecting only a few joints and rarely carried into adulthood; about one-third of all patients develop iridocyclitis

polyarticular arthritis a type of juvenile arthritis similar to adult rheumatoid disease that affects several joints at once; can strike both weight-bearing joints and joints in the hands, jaw, or neck

rheumatism a general term for a condition characterized by inflammation and pain in joints and muscles

rheumatoid arthritis an autoimmune disease in which the joint is damaged and the synovial membrane thickens, producing pannus; rheumatoid arthritis can also affect blood vessels, skin, nerves, muscles, the heart, and the lungs

rheumatoid nodules lumps that develop on the backs of the elbows as a result of rheumatoid arthritis

spondyloarthropathies forms of arthritis primarily affecting the spine

synovial fluid the fluid released by the synovial membrane that lubricates and nourishes joint cartilage

synovial membrane a thin layer of tissue lining the joint that secretes synovial fluid into the joint space

systemic arthritis Still's disease; a severe type of childhood arthritis whose symptoms include a measleslike rash; high fever; fluid build-up around the heart, chest, or abdomen; and painful swelling in the joints; often leaves the child with permanent joint damage and growth problems

tendinitis an inflammation of a tendon

tendons tough bands of white fibrous material that attach bone to muscle

INDEX

PICTURE CREDITS

Mary C. Powers majored in journalism at Indiana University and began her professional career in 1976 as an Associated Press reporter in Indianapolis. She has written about medicine and science for the *Arizona Daily Star* in Tucson, Arizona, and the *Commercial Appeal* in Memphis, Tennessee. Her medical reporting has earned numerous honors, including being named runner-up in 1985 for Scripps Howard Reporter of the Year. She completed her premedical course work at Memphis State and Harvard universities. She spent a year at the Massachusetts Institute of Technology as a Knight Science Journalism Fellow.

Dale C. Garell, M.D., is medical director of California Children Services, Department of Health Services, County of Los Angeles. He is also associate dean for curriculum at the University of Southern California School of Medicine and clinical professor in the Department of Pediatrics & Family Medicine at the University of Southern California School of Medicine. From 1963 to 1974, he was medical director of the Division of Adolescent Medicine at Children's Hospital in Los Angeles. Dr. Garell has served as president of the Society for Adolescent Medicine, chairman of the youth committee of the American Academy of Pediatrics, and as a forum member of the White House Conference on Children (1970) and White House Conference on Youth (1971). He has also been a member of the editorial board of the *American Journal of Diseases of Children.*

C. Everett Koop, M.D., Sc.D., is former Surgeon General, deputy assistant secretary for health, and director of the Office of International Health of the U.S. Public Health Service. A pediatric surgeon with an international reputation, he was previously surgeon-in-chief of Children's Hospital of Philadelphia and professor of pediatric surgery and pediatrics at the University of Pennsylvania. Dr. Koop is the author of more than 175 articles and books on the practice of medicine. He has served as surgery editor of the *Journal of Clinical Pediatrics* and editor-in-chief of the *Journal of Pediatric Surgery.* Dr. Koop has received nine honorary degrees and numerous other awards, including the Denis Brown Gold Medal of the British Association of Paediatric Surgeons, the William E. Ladd Gold Medal of the American Academy of Pediatrics, and the Copernicus Medal of the Surgical Society of Poland. He is a chevalier of the French Legion of Honor and a member of the Royal College of Surgeons, London.